"Walk Humbly
With Thy God..."

Sue Thom

Hosea 14:1-8

SILENT NIGHT

SILENT
NIGHT

SUE THOMAS

WITH S. RICKLY CHRISTIAN

Tyndale House Publishers, Inc., Wheaton, Illinois

Library of Congress Catalog Card Number 90-70377
ISBN 0-8423-5909-5
Printed in the United States of America
09 08 07 06 05 04
12 11 10 9   8   7   6

To Mom and Dad, of course.

The silence could not contain your love.

ACKNOWLEDGMENTS
This story has been in the making for almost forty years. In some respects it's over, and in others it's just beginning. Throughout my entire life I have relied on many people as stepping-stones in my journey in the hearing world. Though it is impossible to acknowledge everyone who has played a part in my life, I wish to thank those who served an important role in shaping this book.

M. E. J., my best friend, got me started on the right path, and Bill Crabb helped pave the way. Bob Coleman gave me the biggest challenge of my life and my biggest hugs, and Pastor Paul Cedar provided wise counsel at that fork in the road. Judy Butler and Joni Eareckson Tada encouraged me again and again to write a book, and Willie Hahn was there in the beginning days. Rick Christian took a chance and believed in me, and I deeply appreciate his tremendous support as my coauthor and friend. Blenda Turnbull Connors, a long-lost childhood friend and neighbor, provided invaluable help with endless hours of transcription. My many friends at Tyndale House Publishers have made these pages a reality, especially Dan Elliott, with his sensitive heart and editorial support, and Timothy Botts, with his gifted design and for allowing me to *see* music.

From the bottom of my heart, I thank you all. I will carry you with me wherever I go.

Sue Thomas

CONTENTS

Even while the sun

is shining brightest,

the storms of life will come;

but through the storm

will come the

white light of promise,

and after the storm

the victory.

W. MARK
SEXSON

INTRODUCTION

For years people told me I had a tremendous, inspiring life story and urged me to write a book. And for years I declined, knowing they merely knew what was on the outside: that I was a deaf woman who had overcome great odds, held a prestigious job with the FBI, and could spin some colorful, often funny, poignant tales about my experiences.

These dear people who encouraged me never fully realized where I had been or what I had done, and for years I was adamant that I would never tell the full story—not even for a million dollars.

I finally relented and worked for nearly two years with author and friend S. Rickly Christian to capture the details of my life—the story beneath the surface. It was a tough, long haul, but I consented because I realized that truth can be learned through another person's life experience.

If in reading about mine, one solitary person finds hope or discovers "the still point" of their turning world, then these long months—and the many, many years that went into living the life you read about within these covers—can be said to have been worth it.

Sue Thomas

SUE THOMAS

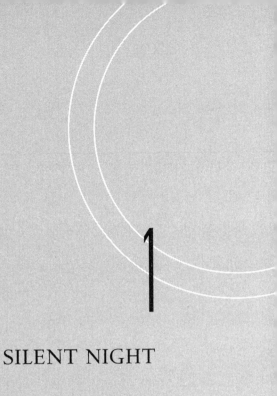

1

SILENT NIGHT

was there when it happened, and it happened to me. But I was too young to remember, and so I rely on the details as they have been passed down by my family.

All families have stories like this, told of a young child who might have, say, split his head on a fall from a tree or down a flight of stairs. Hearing the story for the umpteenth time, the child sits smugly, all the while wondering why he can't remember something that made such an impression on everybody else. He might even reach up and finger the scar that creases his scalp all these years later, yet be unable to recall the headlong spill that cracked his skull in the first place. And so it is with me.

A warm glow of light from the television bathed the living room where I sat with my family, while outside the wind whipped through the trees, kicking at leaves and howling like our little dog Rex did when a raccoon sniffed at the back door. Turning my attention to Rexie, whose head nuzzled against my leg, I listened to his soft breath rise and fall as one of our favorite television programs, "Life with Father," blared in the background.

Less than two years old at the time, I was curled up on the couch with my three older brothers. And then, midway through the program, it happened. Silently, so silently that not even I knew what was happening, my world changed forever.

This life-changing event seemed at first like a small thing. I just thought somebody had turned the television volume down. I flashed my middle brother, Paul, a drop-dead look, thinking he had messed with the knob when I wasn't looking, just as he sometimes snatched cookies off my plate when my back was turned. With a huff, I eased up from the cushy sofa, careful not to disturb Rexie, and turned the volume back up.

When no sound came out, I turned the control higher and higher until my brother jumped up, pushed my hand away, and turned the knob down. I turned it back up, yet the room remained shrouded in silence. With a dagger look, Paul slapped my hand aside and re-adjusted the knob. When I turned it up a third time, Mom abruptly pulled me away. She had a stern look in her eyes, but I knew she was playing because her lips moved silently like the people's on TV.

The moment I touched the knob again, I was suddenly hauled off to my room. Mom continued playing her silent lip game, but each time I tried to walk out of the room she steered me back inside. Finally, abruptly, she picked me up and put me in bed. There I remained for the first long, still, very silent night of the rest of my life.

The next morning Mom snuck into my room after I'd awakened and began playing another kind of game with me that I couldn't understand. She didn't sing to me as she normally did, nor did she ask if I was hungry.

She didn't say anything. She just stood there, moving her lips silently. She kept that up for a long time, sometimes holding my head gently between her hands and moving her lips very slowly, sometimes taking a few steps back and pretending to shout. When I grew disinterested, she pretended to clap her hands, and mouth silent words at the same time. I didn't see the point of that either and eventually wandered over to my toy box. When I looked back up, Mom was gone.

The next thing I knew, I felt a tap on my shoulder and turned around. There was Mom again, standing inches behind me with a whistle in her mouth and her cheeks blown up like balloons. Tears filled her eyes. I just sat there watching her, unable to figure out why she was crying and acting so silly at the same time. Why wouldn't she talk to me normally or even just blow the whistle like she pretended to be doing?

Many years later, when I was old enough to understand, Mom told me that she hadn't been playing games at all but had been speaking and singing to me as she always did. When I didn't respond, she thought it was because my feelings had been hurt the night before. Not even when she told me, "Little Jimmy's coming over," did I show the slightest reaction. Little Jimmy was my friend from across the street, and the chance to play with him would normally have stirred some stand-up-and-holler excitement in me. But I didn't even blink at the news.

Knowing something was wrong, Mom called Little Jimmy's mom, who was a registered nurse. Aunt Ruth, we called her. She was a gentle woman, tall enough to command instant respect, but with hands as soft as a puppy. Mom always called her first when we developed a mysterious fever, got stung by a bee, or came down with chicken pox. When my brother Bobby fell down the stairs and broke his arm, Aunt Ruth was there almost as soon as he hit bottom. She had a calming, authoritative voice and often had us feeling better with no medication other than the assurance that no, we were not dying, or that yes, the virus would pass and we'd be back on our feet within a few days.

This time, however, Aunt Ruth couldn't fix what was wrong with me. Before I knew what was happening, Mom had changed into her pretty blue dress with white polka dots, packed me into Aunt Ruth's borrowed green convertible, and rushed me downtown. By the time we arrived, Mom had worked herself into a perspiring huff as if she'd worked all day in the kitchen. When we got out, she grabbed my hand and raced through the parking lot so fast that I thought my arm would pull right off.

Inside, the building smelled like a doctor's office but looked different. There was just one very large room, divided into what looked like horse stalls. A lady led Mom and me into one of the stalls and lifted me into a metal chair with a padded headrest. Beside me was a light and a table lined with jars of cotton and tongue sticks and thermometers. There was a trash can that opened by stepping on a pedal, as well as a chair for Mom. But she stood beside me, holding my hand tightly as if she thought I'd get up and run away.

There were no curtains to pull, so I could see everybody in the other stalls, and everybody could see me. In the middle of the large room stood a shiny metal table. The woman lying on it had tools of some sort sticking from her ears. The doctor, a tall, gray-haired man with hands like catcher's mitts, moved from stall to stall, looking in people's ears, mouths, and noses. Two people had their heads tilted back with bloody swabs of cotton sticking out of their noses.

On his head the doctor wore a leather band that held a doughnut-shaped mirror. The light was turned on when he looked in people's ears and noses, or when he poked inside the ears of those lying on the big table. His name, I learned later, was Dr. Raymond Hall.

Mom eventually loosened her grip and planted little kisses on my fingers until Dr. Hall came in. He wore a short-sleeved white jacket, dark pants, and a warm, fleshy smile. Placing one of his mitt-sized hands on my shoulder, he immediately began playing silent mouth games with me, just as Mom had done that morning.

When I tired of watching his lips move, he flipped his mirror down over his eye and put a tongue stick in my mouth. Then he stuck a cotton-topped stick down my throat until I gagged, and with another he probed inside my nostrils. When he looked in my ears, I was afraid he'd haul me to the big table and work me over with a screwdriver or whatever that was sticking out of the lady's ears.

I clung to the chair for dear life, but there was nothing really to worry about. When he finished looking and poking and breathing hot air down my neck, he just turned to Mom and shook his head. They said something to each other in the new silent language everybody but me could speak. And then Mom stood up, walked over to my side by the chair, and drew my head tight against her breast. When she stepped back, tears were streaming down her face.

Mom's fears had been confirmed, and she suddenly knew what I was unable to understand. For some inexplicable reason, I was stone-cold deaf. One day I could hear; the next, I was living in a world without sound. And not even the doctor could explain why. As he told Mom that day so many years ago, "Your daughter's hearing is gone. There's nothing there, nothing at all."

When Mom asked if there was anything that could be done, he told her to wait a couple of weeks. Perhaps my hearing would click back on. If it didn't, he said he'd remove my tonsils and adenoids. Maybe that would somehow help. Then he shook our hands and we left.

By the time we reached the car, Mom looked so sad that I started crying too. We sat there in the heat of the sun, clinging to each other and crying until our tears dried up. Then Mom started the car, but it bucked like a wild horse. She tried again, but the car lurched forward and stalled. A nice man finally came over and showed her how to work the pedals, and we got home without Mom crying again.

The next days were a blur of people mouthing silent words to me, banging silent pans together, and clapping silent hands inches from my head, all the while staring at me expectantly. I stared back until they started to cry. Even Dad cried, and I wondered what I had done to make everybody so very, very sad.

Two weeks later, Mom packed a small suitcase for me with four changes of underwear, and Dad loaded me and my suitcase into our big, black Oldsmobile. I sat in the front, between him and Mom, hugging my teddy bear tightly. I was the only one with a suitcase, and I thought maybe they didn't want me anymore. I thought they wanted me to live with somebody else.

When we pulled to a stop in front of a hospital, however, I realized that maybe I was just sick and would not be given away after all. Inside, the halls were smelly clean, and everybody wore white except those who were pushed around in chairs with big wheels. They wore blue nasty gowns. I was taken to a room, my clothes were taken off, and I too was dressed in a nasty gown that showed my bottom.

Then a man wearing green pajamas and green booties came in, loaded me onto a rolling bed, and wheeled me out of my room. My parents followed, carrying my teddy bear. I didn't know where he was taking me and started getting scared, but Mom stopped the rolling bed and gave me my teddy bear. Then she and Dad both gave me a kiss, and the man in green pajamas rolled me through some doors and into a very cold room. Everybody inside the cold room was wearing green pajamas and masks. They put me on a metal table, and then a lady put a cup over my mouth and nose. Suddenly I felt like I wanted to jump up and fly, *really* fly, around the room! Then the lady went fuzzy, and I began floating down a funnel in slow motion. My eyes were heavy as rocks.

When I opened my eyes again, my head ached and I wanted to cry. My mouth was stuffed full of cotton, and I could only breathe through my nose. My parents came in and patted me on the head and moved their lips at me. I tried to smile but thought I would throw up. My throat was on fire, and I hugged Teddy as tightly as I could.

I stayed in the hospital until my clean underwear ran out, and then I went home. Still, there was no sound. When people talked at me, I couldn't hear them. When they smiled or cried, I didn't know what they were smiling or crying about.

As Mom told me later, the surgery to remove my tonsils and adenoids did nothing for my deafness. My only consolation was that I got all the ice cream and sherbet I could eat, even for breakfast. That helped ease my pain and fears, but the shroud of silence continued to envelop me.

The silence began to scare me because everybody seemed to sneak up on me when I least expected it. I became most scared at night, when the silence was compounded by darkness. Unable either to hear or see, I cried silent tears until Mom came and lay down beside me, holding and kissing me until I fell asleep in her arms.

Without Mom nearby, I felt lost. She was my security—the still point of my turning world. I could count on her to remain constant—in what she wore, the way she smelled and combed her hair, how she woke me in the morning with a smile, and the way she curled her fingers in my hair when she hugged me close. I loved and trusted her with all of my heart, and I held onto the hem of her dress when she moved from room to room.

Mom took me to Dr. Hall's office twice weekly. On one of the visits he put me on the cold, metal table in the middle of the big room. Five other people held me down and tilted my head back until my chin pointed straight up. Then Dr. Hall put on big, heavy gloves and opened a metal box from which he pulled what looked like knitting needles. I learned later they were radium sticks. By inserting them up my nostrils, he thought he could possibly restore my hearing.

The needles were rough and prickly, but I couldn't kick because I was pinned to the table. The further he inserted them up my nose, the more it hurt. My slightest movement caused fireworks in my head. With tears clouding my sight, I looked up at Mom who was holding my arm down. *Why is she letting the doctor hurt me?*

The radium treatments didn't restore my hearing, and they were discontinued when small lumps broke out all over my body. Despite the failure of that and every other method tried by the doctors in Youngstown, Ohio, my parents held out hope that specialists in bigger cities might, just *might*, be able to somehow turn my ears back on. And so we traveled to Cleveland, Pittsburgh, Nashville, Buffalo, and New York. My father, a housepainter, took extra jobs to pay for the trips, and he accompanied me and Mom whenever possible.

In those faraway cities, the scenes from Youngstown were repeated again and again. I went into a small booth. The doctors looked up my nose, down my throat, and in my ears. Then they put earphones on me that looked like big, brown salad bowls and felt like a vise. I played with toys while the doctors fiddled with knobs on their equipment, and my parents intently watched my face for any sign that I might possibly, hopefully, prayerfully pick up the slightest, smallest hint of a sound. However, audiograms always registered a sound loss of 100 to 110 decibels. Because my loss was more than 80 decibels, I was considered to be legally, profoundly deaf. Not only was I deaf to people and animals, but also to airplane engines, honking horns, and screaming sirens.

The permanence of my deafness was confirmed with another instrument, a metal headpiece that was strapped around my skull. A small button on the end sat against the bone behind my ear. Many years later, Mom said it determined that I had nerve deafness rather than bone deafness. The latter can be surgically restored, but nothing in medical science can restore the nerve.

About that time astronaut Alan Shepard underwent an operation that restored a temporary hearing loss, enabling him to return to space. His was not nerve deafness, but my parents didn't want to overlook anything and so arranged for the same surgery. Afterward, the surgeon told my parents that all my critical ear components—the eardrum, malleus, incus, tympanic membrane, stapes, eustachian tube, semicircular canals, vestibule, cochlea, and internal auditory meatus—were all in working order. All, that is, except for a tiny hair of a nerve that relayed electrical signals from the ear to the brain. It had developed a short, which the doctors could neither explain nor fix. Nevertheless, they did for me what they did with the astronaut: installed small shunts into my inner ear, hoping the increased oxygen supply would stimulate and activate the nerve. But this, too, proved futile—a valiant effort, but nothing more than chasing after rainbows.

The visits to the various clinics became a ritual of sorts. After the tests, the doctor came in. With one hand he patted me on the head; the other offered me a lollipop. And then he turned and spoke to my parents. My dad would reach over and hold Mom close, and soon they both would be crying. I never understood why they cried, and I offered them my sucker to make them happy. But that only made them cry more.

At last my parents were convinced I was permanently trapped in a world without sound. Nonetheless, they didn't give up. They made a solemn vow to each other: to help make me as much a part of the hearing world as possible. They didn't want me to remain forever outside of their world looking in. They wanted me to share in it. That commitment led straight to the doorstep of the Youngstown Hearing and Speech Center and a meeting with the Iron Witch.

2

THE IRON WITCH

was three years old when I first walked up the altarlike steps of the Youngstown Hearing and Speech Center. Located across town from our southside suburb, it looked like a dark and foreboding castle. Black crows lined the roof. I gripped Mom's hand till my knuckles turned white as she turned the knob and pushed against the weathered, towering door. It opened slowly into a room with vast stone walls and a brick fireplace that only partially cut the chill.

As we stepped inside, my eyes roamed: thick Persian rugs on the floor . . . heavy woods outlining every doorway and window . . . a beamed ceiling with cobwebs high in the corners. But what most attracted my attention was an enormous mirror mounted on the far wall. When I looked back at Mom, she was talking to a stiff, gray-haired woman. Known to others as Miss May Vetterle, she became the Iron Witch to me.

She was a thin, frail woman, with the delicate features of a teacup. But the look on her face was that of an army general, able to pierce me and the cold stone walls at my back. She stuck out her veiny hand for me to shake, but it wasn't a normal handshake because she didn't let go.

She led me by the hand down the hall away from Mom and into a sprawling room that felt refrigerator cold. Though the walls were painted a warm sunshine yellow, the chill rose out of the hardwood floor, seeped into my shoes, and crawled up my legs until I was covered with goose bumps.

Miss Vetterle's metal-rimmed glasses were perched perfectly on the bridge of her hawkish nose, and her gray hair was frozen in a light wave by half a can of Aqua Net spray. Her shoes were thick-heeled and black, and her skirt, blouse, and jacket had razor-sharp creases.

Hearing-impaired herself, she never took her jacket off because it camouflaged her body aid—a metal amplifier strapped to her chest and wired to an ear piece. Ramrod straight with piercing hazel eyes, she seemed allergic to smiles and laughter. Her allergy was contagious because it was impossible to even think about smiling in her presence.

Miss Vetterle let me play for a few minutes with the toys and puppets that were shelved along the wall. Then she steered me to the front of the room and sat me in a small chair that faced the big mirror. Sitting beside me, she pulled an apple from a bag on the floor and began moving her lips at me in the mirror. I stared at her and wondered what she was saying. She pointed at it and moved her lips again.

I reached out to take the apple, but she drew it away. That seemed like a mean thing to do, and I almost started to cry. But then she raised my chin so I was looking back in the mirror. She was again moving her lips and pointing at the apple. I wiped my eyes and looked away, unable to understand why she kept teasing me.

Finally she put it back in her bag and pulled out a cookie. Then she repeated what she'd done with the apple, pointing at it and moving her lips. I wanted the cookie more than I wanted the apple, but when I reached for it, she pulled it out of reach and shook her head. I did cry then, blurting, "Cookie, cookie, cookie," through my tears. At that point she stroked my head and nodded vigorously. She held the cookie back up and, pointing to it, moved her lips again. Her lips said, "Cookie," which was what I wanted, so I said, "Cookie," too. She really nodded then, and her face looked like I had done something right.

She then took my hand and placed my palm gently on her throat. I looked at her in the mirror, unable to figure out what she was doing. Her lips were still saying, "Cookie," so I repeated the word, and then she said it again and again, "Cookie, cookie, cookie."

Suddenly I was aware that her throat was vibrating. I felt it in my fingers every time her lips moved! I glanced at her throat, and her face brightened as if she knew that I knew her throat was vibrating. Just then she took my hand off her throat and moved it to mine, and when I said, "Cookie," I felt vibrations in my throat as well!

At that point, Miss Vetterle gave me a grandma pat on the head and handed me the cookie. I didn't know if this was a trick or not, so I looked up at her and said, "Cookie?" She nodded and repeated the word back to me. And then her lips moved again, as if to say it was all right to eat it. Hesitantly, I moved it toward my mouth, expecting her to snatch it away. But she didn't, and I gobbled it into my mouth in one bite.

When I was finished, she wiped the chocolate chip smudges off my face and then pulled a long white candle out of her bag. Holding it up before the mirror, she pointed at it and moved her lips. I looked up and said, "Candle?" She nodded and moved my fingers to her throat. I held on but could feel no vibrations. She promptly withdrew my hand and shook it until my fingers flapped around like the ears of the rabbit puppet. When she put my fingers back on her throat, she held my wrist so my fingers would rest more lightly. And then her lips said, "Candle," and I again felt her throat vibrate. Shifting my fingers to my own throat, I said, "Cookie," but Miss Vetterle didn't like that. She pointed at the candle, and so I said, "Candle," instead. She nodded her head. I repeated the word, and she nodded again.

Next she moved my palm inches from her mouth and blew on my fingers as if they were candles. I blew on my other hand, and she nodded. Then she mouthed, "Candle," into my open hand. I felt a slight puff of breath as she spoke the word, but not as much as when she blew. I tried the same on my palm and felt the same puff. She again seemed to know that I knew about the puff, and though she didn't smile, her dark hazel eyes brightened.

Glancing at her watch, she then pulled the apple back out of her bag. This time I knew her lips were saying, "Apple," and I knew I was to repeat it. Then I felt her throat and mine vibrate and felt the puff of "apple" from her mouth and mine. After playing this game for a few minutes, she handed me the apple, gave my head a pat, and then led me back to where I'd left Mom.

Mom wasn't there right away, but when she rounded the corner a few minutes later, I ran up and showed her the apple Miss Vetterle had given me. She was all smiles, and she let me hold onto her leg as the two of them talked briefly. On the way home, she drove with her arm around me as I savored my apple, bite by sweet bite.

On subsequent visits, we repeated much the same procedure. We started with a short playtime, followed by repeating words at each other in front of the mirror. At first the words were easy: *doll, car, dog, banana, finger.* The sessions became more difficult when she tried to teach me more abstract words such as *hungry, love, bad, good.*

And then, just as I figured out that we were merely playing a game of kiddy charades and I only had to guess the word she acted out or showed on the picture card, the rules changed. One day, out of the blue, Miss Vetterle made me play a different game, which wasn't a game at all. She flashed cards at me with pictures on them that I'd not seen before: letters of the alphabet, as I later discovered they were called.

Week after miserable, endless week we reviewed those letters, and I tried to repeat the sound each of them made. But how could I do that when I'd never before heard their names or sounds? How do you learn to say the letter *A* for the first time? Miss Vetterle shook her head again and again as I verbalized what I thought she was saying. But every attempt with "ah" or "ahee" or a hundred other variations drew no more support from her than if I'd said *kangaroo.*

My tongue had to be held at just the right angle, my lips formed in just the right position, my vibrations controlled at just the right level, and my breath released in just the right measure, and even then—even if I happened by helpless chance to stumble upon the correct pronunciation, I couldn't remember what I'd done so as to repeat the miracle. And that was just the first letter. I had yet to work my way through the mine fields of *G, H, Q, X,* and so many, many more.

I tried and tried and kept on trying to get it right, to hold the many parts of my mouth in the exact position in which Miss Vetterle held hers, but the successes came so infrequently that it seemed impossible to earn her approval. Whatever happened to her nods and grandma pats and cookie treats? Why couldn't she smile and acknowledge the impossibility of the task? Would she next expect me to sprout wings and fly? Why couldn't the awful, horrible, Miss Meany Vetterle just leave me alone?

With the absence of approval and passage of time, I grew increasingly rebellious. Sitting in the chair, I made faces at Miss Vetterle in the mirror. When she ignored me and continued the lesson, I watched her with the cold, dead eyes of a statue. When she put her hand on my throat to measure my vibrations, I reached up and jerked it away. Wanting no part of the lesson, I got up and stomped over to the toy shelf. She followed on my heels, taking my hand and leading me back to the chair. If I pulled away, she grabbed me by anything she could hold onto and forced me back.

This Iron Witch of a woman with the frozen gray hair and the thick black shoes began to scare me. I felt caged in her big, cold room with the giant mirror that seemed to mock my every motion, and I wanted Mom. But when I raced for the door, only to be dragged back, I felt as frightened as a little animal caught in one of my brother's traps.

Fighting for freedom, I kicked and screamed, clawed her face, elbowed her ribs, dug my heel into her shoe, socked her chest, and even pulled her hair. But she never broke, not even when I ran screaming toward the door. No matter what happened, she never slapped or spanked me. She watched from her post by the mirror, making no effort to move, but staring at me like a hunter with her cold, hazel eyes. Her eyes penetrated me, and I froze on the spot, sobbing uncontrollably, unable to run or escape out the door. Then she simply rose from her chair, threw back her shoulders, and marched over to my side. Grabbing me with a vise-like grip, she led me back to the mirror, held up another card or placed my hand on her throat, and we began the process all over again.

After a year of therapy in the big, yellow room, Miss Vetterle switched our sessions to the basement, which was down a dark, steep stairwell and through a passageway that was so narrow we had to walk single file. It was dingy and dungeon cold, and I knew nobody could hear my screams from down there. Throw rugs were spread across the concrete floors to break the chill, but dampness hung in the air and went straight to my bones. Like the upstairs room, the dungeon also had a sprawling mirror, in front of which I spent endless hours perfecting my ability to speak, read lips, and battle the Iron Witch.

One day after a long and grueling session, I was surprised when I got home to discover that Miss Vetterle had cloned herself—in the person of my very own dear mother! But Mom was not so dear when she spent the afternoon reviewing everything Miss Vetterle had taught me earlier. Perched in front of her vanity dresser mirror with me at her side, she proceeded through the session in the same step-by-step order, and when I fussed or ran she gently led me back without reaching for the fly swatter.

I wondered how she suddenly became a therapist herself and knew the exact techniques used in the dungeon room. I discovered her secret one day when we arrived early for a session. Miss Vetterle relayed word for Mom to take me downstairs. I thought I needed to lead her, but she knew right where she was going—not to the dungeon room, but to the room next door where two other mothers were gazing intently through a smokey window.

I looked where they were looking and was surprised to see Miss Vetterle a few feet away on the other side, working with another child just as she worked with me! She held an apple in her hand, but the girl had tears in her eyes. I knew she didn't understand, so I walked up to the glass and mouthed, "Apple." When she didn't respond, I waved and tried to get her attention, but still she didn't see me. Then I realized the glass I was looking through was, on the other side, a mirror. I was looking through the back side of the dungeon room mirror! I could see them, but they couldn't see me!

I wanted to jump up and down and tell somebody about my discovery, but I didn't know what to say or how to say it. I was so excited, but Mom kept motioning me to shush.

When my turn came to enter the dungeon room, I felt different, more grown up. I was filled with a new power of awareness and knowledge, like Eve after she sampled the apple in Eden. I suddenly knew it wasn't just me and Miss Vetterle in the room, but there were others who, like ghosts, spied on us from the secret room.

So I did what any youngster with this new awareness would do. I jumped up from Miss Vetterle's side and began waving at the mirror. I didn't know whether just Mom was in the secret room or whether it was full, whether nobody waved back or whether everybody waved. And so I kept waving. Then I stuck my thumbs in my ears and made clown faces and hopped around Miss Vetterle on one foot and finally walked smack up to the mirror and put my eye against the glass. I could still see nothing, but that didn't mean there weren't dozens of people inside the secret room—maybe smoking cigarettes or having a party or dancing or, for that matter, even running around naked!

Then I began to feel stupid, knowing Mom was doing none of those things. She was probably just watching me and thinking how silly and dumb I was. Wishing I could disappear on the spot, I turned around and walked very slowly back to my chair. When I sat down and glanced up at Miss Vetterle, I was shocked to see the corner of her mouth twitching. I darted another look. She was fighting back a *smile!* Good ol' stiff-haired Miss Vetterle actually knew how to smile! I was dumfounded. It was a bigger discovery than the secret room. She wasn't entirely a witch after all!

As the weeks and months of therapy turned to years, the individual letters of the alphabet came alive. Vowels had heavy vibrations that were deep and throaty and resonant. *A, E, I, O, U*—each felt dynamic and friendly when pronounced. They had a strong presence, and I was as comfortable in their company as with a neighborhood companion. Consonants such as *S, P,* and *F,* on the other hand, were airy and lightweight. They were mere wisps of breath, as elusive as a desert mirage.

Vowels were also easier to see. In pronouncing an *I,* I saw in the mirror how my jaw dropped and the skin relaxed at the side of my mouth. Its vibration was low in my throat. With an *E,* the corners of my mouth tightened slightly and the vibration was higher. Split the difference and I had an *A.* With *U,* my lips puckered and the vibrations, coming more from the sides of my throat, were longer.

In the absence of strong vibrations, I felt sounds most prominently in my nasal cavity. The more I felt in my nose, the more sense I had of actually talking. But Miss Vetterle shook her head no, teaching me that when I *felt* I was speaking most clearly, I actually sounded like I had a cold. Slowly, painfully, I began to understand that the key to good speech was not feeling anything at all.

Because of the difficulty of feeling an *S,* I never liked to say my name, Susan. Thomas was much easier. However, Miss Vetterle insisted I learn to pronounce my first name. Week after week, she held my hand in front of her mouth. My palm was the target for the little *S-* puff of air, which slipped out of her mouth in a downward slant. *"Esssss. Esssss. Esssss,"* she repeated again and again. And then she moved my hand to my own mouth and had me duplicate the downward draft.

"Ethhhhh. Ethhhhh. Ethhhhh," I struggled, only to have her shake her head and repeat the exercise.

As I progressed with my therapy, Miss Vetterle sometimes held my mouth wide open so she could teach me how to move my lips and tongue. To learn proper enunciation and articulation, I had to exaggerate movements. Tongue twisters were supposed to help, but all the while my tongue felt like a big wad of cotton in my mouth: "Thhe . . . thhells . . . thhea . . . thhellth . . . by . . . the . . . thheathhore." Like a beached whale, my tongue could barely move.

The sound of *F* was nearly as maddening, and I found it next to impossible to differentiate the word *fan* from *fun*. The words looked the same, as did *three* and *tree*. Because the difference could not be felt or seen, I learned to rely on sentence structure. I knew that somebody was talking about a *three*-year old, not a *tree*-year-old. But without the context of the sentence, I was lost.

Differentiating between *C, Z, T,* and *D* was equally difficult. A *D* had a very slight hint of outward lip movement, with a lower, deeper vibration than a *T,* which was short and straightforward. But I needed a stethoscope and magnifying glass to notice the subtle variations.

When I turned five, I made my debut as a public speaker before supporters of the Youngstown Hearing and Speech Center. Dressed in my prettiest pink Sunday dress, I was ushered to the front of a Youngstown hall. A stranger led me toward the podium and helped me stand on a chair so I could see.

"My name is Susan Thomas," I began, wondering if others could hear my heart pounding. "I am five years old. Miss Vetterle is my teacher. I live in Youngstown, Ohio."

My tongue flopped around inside my mouth like a fish on a hook. But when I stopped, everybody clapped. I turned around and looked to see what they were clapping for, but nobody was there. When it finally struck me that they were clapping for me, I scampered down off the chair and made a giggling, embarrassed dash into Mom's arms. Standing at her side was a Miss Vetterle I'd never seen before. Her piercing eyes were radiant, and her outstretched hand was friendly. Mom set me down on the ground, and I took a hesitant step forward. Reaching out, I gave her hand a quick shake, and then did something I'd never done before. I looked up at her and smiled.

I was overjoyed when, after three years of therapy, Miss Vetterle told my parents that she could do no more for me. At that point I had mastered the basics of lipreading and speech, but my voice was still very nasal, loud, and monotonal. She suggested they try other avenues of therapy, including more advanced voice and drama lessons.

After my therapy with her ended, I never wanted to set foot inside the center or see her again. However, I had trouble avoiding her at the summer county fair, where she conducted free hearing tests. Mom always dragged me over to say hi, but that's all I said. When I was big enough to avoid being dragged, I refused to go near. The years of learning to speak were just too painful and the memories too raw. Times when I wanted to run and play and climb had been spent instead before the large mirror in the dungeon room. I didn't understand why I had to work so hard at what came naturally to most children.

At the time, I thought Miss Vetterle was kin to Attila the Hun, but I eventually realized she was an incredible woman, perhaps even a saint. When I was old enough and mature enough for that to sink in, Miss Vetterle had moved to California. And so I never expressed my appreciation for her unwavering commitment that enabled me to speak. When I had the chance, I never spoke up. It took years before I realized the selfless commitment it took for her to find fulfillment in work that was monotonous and repetitious, and where the results were not seen for years.

When I later tried to track her down and thank her for helping me become a part of the hearing world, I was told she was dead. I can only imagine how the angels sang when this particular saint was ushered home. As for me, I cried like a baby.

Her picture hangs in my office today as a daily reminder of the support she provided when I least appreciated it. All these years later, it is a small tribute. But it's my way of saying thank you to the woman who, through dogged and selfless determination, enabled dreams to be fulfilled that I didn't even know I had.

3

GAMES BROTHERS PLAY

was born and grew up in the nickel-and-dime outskirts of Youngstown, Ohio, a virtual ghost town filled with the carcasses of old, rusty steel mills. It was as if one day the sun didn't rise in that one stretch of country between Pittsburgh and Cleveland: all the people packed their bags, and the once-bustling city just folded up. Our home in Boardman was pure country. We had no running water or sewer, just a pump and septic tank. Nobody had fences, so our front and back yards seemed to stretch as far as I could see, eventually merging on the horizon into dense woods.

Rimmed with giant blue spruce trees, our yard was a combination football field and garden war zone. On a piece of an acre behind the house, we raised a grocery store variety of vegetables, from corn to winter potatoes. Our family lived off that garden, but I loved it most for its big, juicy beefeater tomatoes, which were better than snowballs or water balloons in a backyard fight. I stockpiled an arsenal of beefeaters and got no bigger thrill than scoring a direct hit on one of my attacking brothers. That seldom happened, of course, because my brothers were seven, ten, and thirteen years older than I. As the baby of the family, I was more often the target.

One of my favorite trees, the crab apple, supplemented the ammo supply. In the summer, it sprouted hundreds of little apples that, unlike beefeaters, hurt when they hit. The base of that tree was, in my young mind, as historic and strategic as Guadalcanal. The brother who controlled that golden spot controlled the world. As the underdog, I wisely left world affairs in his hands . . . or risked being sent *yeeooow*ing into the house in pain.

The long summer days were the best days of all. The boys and I played outside until the sky turned from blue to pink to purple, and then we captured lightning bugs by the jarful or ate watermelon and spit seeds off the back porch. Rex was always at my side, barking at the bugs I'd catch or lapping up dropped bits of watermelon.

When the summer sky got really dark and I was unable to see faces to read lips, my world closed in around me and I was enveloped by loneliness. I'd stumble through the darkness just to be close to somebody, but I always felt as if a black curtain separated me from others. This developed into a fear of darkness, which could only be solved by retreating into the house, where I'd watch the others dart back and forth beneath the shadows of the moon.

The climax of summer was the Fourth of July, which my family celebrated with a huge barbecue, followed by games of football, baseball, badminton, and croquet. Afterward, we'd all sit on blankets in the yard and watch fireworks rocket skyward from the nearby park.

Sometimes my parents' square dance friends came over. I enjoyed this because there were always lots of long-necked bottles sitting around in the grass. I wandered from blanket to blanket, chair to chair, swigging the last swallows from dozens of these near-empty bottles. It made me feel cool and warm all at the same time and made the adults hoot with laughter.

At one of these parties, one of the men started dancing by himself in the middle of the group. Laughing so hard he just about fell over, he then tried to get another man's wife to sit in his lap. I thought it was all pretty funny until the two men stood up nose to nose and got red in the face. Push led to shove, and before long, fists were flying and they were rolling in the grass like little boys, trying to beat the bejabbers out of each other. It was all the others could do to hold them down and pin their arms to keep them from turning each other into hamburger.

Afterward a lot of mean looks were exchanged, and if looks could kill, you'd have called it a bloodbath. I didn't hear the words people exchanged, but I had eyes to see the guests hurriedly pack their things and leave.

I didn't think much about it other than to wonder why the woman's husband got so uptight about her sitting on somebody else's lap. At my age, I couldn't understand why adults made such a big deal out of everything. I figured they should have just sat down, opened a few more long-necked bottles, and let the man laugh and dance and play his silly lap game.

I didn't know what key to the puzzle I was missing, but it was obvious the adults understood something I didn't. It was as if I kept adding two plus two and, again and again, coming up with three. All of my childhood was that way. I felt like I was outside a store, peering through the giant, plate-glass window, and not having the foggiest idea what was going on inside.

At that young age, I participated as best as I could in the hearing world—sometimes with mixed results. One of my favorite games was hide 'n' seek. Because of my deafness, I often hid with my youngest brother, Bobby, who was seven years older than I.

Tall and lanky, with hazel eyes and a brown crew cut, Bobby was constantly wiping a drippy nose or fighting the flu. Though we all got chicken pox, the disease nearly killed him. He played baseball and football with the neighborhood kids but seemed to operate in slow motion. It was as if he was still anticipating the hike, long after the ball was in motion and the other players were sprinting down field on their assigned routes.

Because he lived in the shadows cast by our older brothers, Paul and Billy, I was about the only person he could dominate. While playing hide 'n' seek, he'd shush me quiet and then get this big-eyed look on his face, alerting me to approaching footsteps. Instantly, I'd freeze solid as stone and squeeze my eyes shut. My breaths would come in spurts, and I'd grip his hand till my fingers tingled. After several long minutes of being a statue, I'd feel a tap on my shoulder. Opening my eyes, I'd see my brother's laughing face and his lips telling me that he was just kidding; nobody was coming.

To him it was all a big joke. But to me it was serious business. Just as I'd catch my breath and relax, his body would snap tense and his finger would dart to his lips.

He thought it was the funniest thing, the way I'd go rigid and take tiny breaths.

When I hid alone, my body was tense with nervous excitement. The person looking for me could have been two blocks away, but because I couldn't hear, I always thought they were just a few steps away. I'd hunker down in my little hiding spot, my heart in my throat, never hearing the call to freedom, "All ye, all ye, in come free." As a result, I'd be stuck—in the back of a car, inside the garage, or behind the neighbor's woodshed—for hours without hardly blinking, only to finally sneak out and discover the other players had gone home to lunch or were well into another game.

Through this process, I began to understand that I was different from most other people, but it never sank in to the point that I *felt* different. My parents and doctors told me I was deaf, and tests proved it. But as a child, that never translated to where I actually *believed* I was different, not deep down at the emotional level where differences are really felt. When playing hide 'n' seek, I got excited and sometimes hid too long, not knowing the game was over. I had jokes played on me, but so did everybody else. Maybe I was different, but not *that* different.

Like the baby of any family, I got my fair share of love and attention, if not more. But I also endured my due portion of sibling abuse from my brothers. Being deaf granted me no special privileges.

My middle brother, Paul, who was ten years older than I, had a great love of the woods. Sometimes he even ditched school, jumping off the bus at the first stop past our house and heading off to check his traps along the stream. The outdoors was his sanctuary; hunting, his religion.

I often watched as he headed off, lugging seven or eight bear claw traps over his shoulder. He was skinny as a board and didn't have an ounce of meat on his body. His chiseled Abe Lincoln face was accented by a shock of the curliest hair east of the Missouri River. My eyes followed him until he disappeared into the far stand of trees.

I ached to go with him, but he wanted his kid sister along about as much as a splinter under his thumbnail. I begged him to take me with him. "I'll be quiet!" I promised, but he usually said no. Once when he was fifteen and I was five, I cried long and loud enough that Mom forced him to take me. But he took off at a fast pace, and I had to sprint to catch up.

"Shut up!" he snapped, moving his lips in slow motion when I finally caught up. I knew he was mad because his eyes squinched and his forehead wrinkled up like the bark of an old tree.

"I didn't say anything," I protested.

"You're breathing like an old horse and scaring all the animals away!"

I quickly scanned the fields and trees. If it was a ten-point buck he was looking for, he was right; there wasn't one around. I shrugged it off. "There's a birdie," I said triumphantly, pointing toward a nearby tree.

"I said to shut your mug!" he huffed, balling up his fist as if he were about to rearrange my face. "You're shouting! Shouting about a stupid old crow!"

"I'm not shouting!"

He threw up his hands. "How would you even know?"

"I'm telling Mom when we get home," I said.

"Say anything and I'll knock you flat!"

"You wouldn't dare!"

"Would too!"

"Would not!"

He stuck his nose right into my face so I couldn't miss his lips. "Another word, and I'll skin you alive. Rip the skin right off your face. I swear I will. Then I'll stuff it with kitty litter and mount you on a tree to scare off the crows."

I didn't understand everything he said, but the look in his eyes was pure, unadulterated, premeditated evil, so I hushed up and stayed a safe three paces behind him.

We hadn't gone very far when he suddenly whipped around and flashed a dragon face. "Can't you walk any quieter?"

"Quieter?"

"Quieter!"

"I'm on tiptoes."

He looked as if he were going to bite me. "There, right now, you're like a cow crashing through the trees. Lighten up, would you!"

"Huh?"

"You don't walk normal. I'm out here quiet as an Indian, and you're tripping over roots, breaking twigs, and huffing like a horse! Normally I see deer and all kinds of great things, but with you tagging along all I see is a stupid old crow."

Tears suddenly stung my eyes. He was right. Unknowingly, I had totally ruined his time in the woods.

Thinking back on the few times I'd gone with him, I never saw him bring any animals back. Without me, he always bagged something—a fox, raccoon, or squirrel—which he then brought home to mount.

One time Paul headed farther into the woods than normal and asked Mom to pick him up at a certain place four hours later. At the appointed hour, I jumped in the car with her, squirming with excitement to think Paul might have shot something really big, such as a deer or an elk.

When we reached our designated rendezvous point, Paul was waiting with his gun cradled over his arm and his gunny sack draped over his shoulder. Because he obviously had not shot anything big, I didn't embarrass him by asking what was in the bag.

Paul threw the bag in the back of the car and jumped in. The car suddenly began to stink. I thought the smell was just Paul, but when I rolled down the window, it didn't go away. It was so strong I could taste it.

"You must have shot a skunk," I finally said. I held my nose and glanced at Mom. Her lips began to move.

"A skunk!" she said.

I didn't catch what Paul said, or what she said back. But when we got home, she wouldn't allow him to bring the bag inside. Though he skinned and mounted the animal outside, Paul brought the smell in on his hands, and the house stunk for days afterward.

Killing always generated strong emotion in me, but I never saw Paul's animals until he had them strung upside down and began skinning. By that point, the animal was a puddle of blood and a stinking, red bulge of muscles and tissue, with folds of fur pulled down around its head. I could barely recognize what it was, and the next time I saw it was after mounting. So I missed the warm, fuzzy stage where the animal's long eyelashes and inviting but lifeless eyes would have made me think somebody's pet had just been murdered.

As a little girl, I often walked up and stared at his stuffed foxes, raccoons, and birds. He had them scattered around the house, on walls, atop dressers and tables, in closets. For fear the animals could still bite, I never touched them, though I stared deep into their amber or chocolate eyes from arm's length. I kept my distance when night fell because the light from the moon or a table lamp created horrific shadows, turning pheasants into flying monsters, small fish into sharks, raccoons into wolves, and foxes into bears.

Paul worked in the fruit cellar, a section of the basement that Dad allowed him to use as a taxidermy workshop. Sometimes when I got up the courage and could stand the stench, I watched him from the doorway. But he always knew I was there and would jerk open the door suddenly.

"Go away!" he'd snap.

"It's a free world," I'd respond, using one of the lines I'd seen him use when confronted by our oldest brother, Billy.

"I'm warning you . . ."

"This is my house too."

"You want some greasy, grimy goose guts smeared in your face?"

"I'm telling."

"Scram or I'll make you eat it!"

"You wouldn't."

"Oh, yeah?" And with that he would dash across the room, grab some bloody mess of entrails off the floor, and chase me up the basement stairs as I screamed for Mom to save me.

When Paul got especially mad, he'd threaten to stuff Rexie and turn him into a doorstop. Little Rex was of indeterminate—or, as I preferred, all-American—breed. He just showed up in our yard one day when I was two, and though everybody in our family claimed him as their own, I knew he was mine. From the start, Rex understood me better than anyone else. Through tough times, in the absence of friends, he was my anchor. I would throw my arms around his little black body, knowing he understood all my problems.

"Get your cruddy, smelly body out of my room, or Rex is history!" Paul's lips sometimes threatened. "Touch my mitt again, and Rex hangs on the mantle!" he'd say on other occasions.

One day Rex disappeared into the woods and didn't return. I cried for two days straight. A few days later I looked out the window and saw Rex trailing Paul home from the woods. The dog was limping. I bolted for the door and ran outside to snatch him into my arms. His paw was matted with dried blood and mud.

"Stupid dog," Paul snapped as I ran up.

"Stupid!" I cried, kneeling down as hot tears ran down my cheeks. "Poor, poor Rex. Where have you been, Rexie, poor little Rexie? And what's wrong with your paw? How did you hurt your little paw?"

"Stupid dog was caught in one of my traps," Paul said, his dagger eyes flashing. "Scared off all the animals I would've caught."

At that moment, I cursed my brother straight to the blast furnaces of hell, where I imagined he would writhe in hot boiling oil. I hated him.

For two days Rex slept off the accident in front of the fireplace and refused to move. I sat beside him, my legs cushioning his head, my tears falling into his soft fur, my fingers stroking his ears. I'd almost lost my best friend. This prompted an uncomfortable mixture of anger and thankfulness. I secretly hoped Paul would step in one of his own traps. But I also felt exhilarated that Rex was still alive, able to breathe, flick his ears, wag his tail, and watch me with his big brown eyes. The tugs of emotion nearly broke my heart.

I was surprised several days later when Paul stopped beside the fireplace where Rex and I sat. He gently stroked Rexie's head, all the time repeating, "You poor boy. Poor, poor Rex."

He nudged my arm and I looked up. "Susie, I've decided to get rid of the traps."

His lips were moving too fast. "Traps . . . what?" I said.

"No more traps. I am throwing them out."

I felt a lump rise in my throat.

"They're trouble."

I nodded.

"I'll still do my taxidermy, but I'll use my gun instead of traps."

"Gun?"

"Yes, no more traps."

"Rex could have died," I said.

"There won't be no more accidents. I promise." He reached over and gave my head a pat. A few moments later, he stood, hiked up his pants, and smiled at me like I couldn't ever remember him smiling before. It made me want to hug my brother, but I knew I didn't dare. I just looked away and stroked Rex a little faster.

To cool off in the summer, my brothers and I dragged out the hose and sprinkler, or else Mom carted us off to the city pool. My brothers enjoyed swimming at nearby lakes and ponds, but I never went in. I couldn't see the bottom, and they told me the murky depths were filled with scaled, big-toothed monsters that ate little girls and neighbor's stray cats and dogs.

Paul and I also fished a lot in the summer. Within a short distance from home was an abundance of catfish, trout, and some bass. To get worms for bait, we'd water our lawn in the afternoon. Upon nightfall, we'd grab the flashlights and search the grass for night crawlers. We'd save them in a bucket of dirt, topped with a layer of ice. And what we didn't spot, the robins would polish off the following day.

It was cool in the nearby woods, and we'd follow a trickle of a stream until it emptied into a small lake. I was careful not to stray too far behind my brother. He always said to hurry up or the bogeyman would get me. I didn't exactly know what a bogeyman was, but according to my brother, it came out of the woods at night and sometimes even hid under my bed.

Any doubts I may have had about its existence were laid to rest late one afternoon as dusk approached. My brothers, who were working in the garden, told me to run over to the home of a neighbor, Jake Levine, to borrow a small spade.

"It's in Jake's toolshed," Paul said. "He ain't home now, but it's OK."

"I'm not going alone," I said, noting the darkening sky. Sometimes I'd hidden behind the toolshed when we played hide 'n' seek, but I'd never ventured inside by myself. Nor was I about to with nightfall approaching.

"Oh, I'll go with the baby," Paul groused. "I don't want the bogeyman to get her."

"I'm not afraid of the bogeyman," I said.

"Then go by yourself."

"You come too—just in case."

"Sure." Paul nodded, winking at Bobby and Billy. "You never know."

About halfway there, we were joined by my other two brothers. "Just in case," they said.

We crossed the Levine's broad stretch of grass, ducked through some bushes, and then came up on the shed. It nestled beneath a spreading oak near the back of their lot. When we were about three yards from the shed, Paul stopped suddenly, and I ran smack into his back.

"Shhhh!" he said, "I hear a noise."

"What kind of noise?" I asked.

"A bogeyman kind."

"Where?"

"Inside, dummy!" His face looked like he was shouting, but I knew he had to be whispering. I grabbed the edge of his shirt and held on tightly. He waited a long moment, his head cocked, then took another step.

"Heck, it was probably just the wind," he said, reaching for the handle. I wasn't so sure.

Pulling the door open, Paul stepped quickly inside and fumbled for the light string dangling from the ceiling. I followed on his heels, with Bob and Billy trailing behind.

Out of the corner of my eye, I noticed a sudden motion. My heart jumped. I glanced over at Paul. His face was bug-eyed. Bob and Billy were scrambling out the door fast. Their faces read fear. Everybody was pushing and shoving, and I was trapped in the middle. I still didn't know what the commotion was, but I wasn't going to hang around and ask. Everything was a blur of shadows. Suddenly I felt a webbed, leathery thing on my shoulder. I whipped around and screamed.

Looming toward me was a mass of darkness. It looked part human, part reptile. Its head was gigantic and caged; its paws, big as catcher's mitts; its belly, fat and orange; its legs, covered with shiny scales. I screamed again and stampeded through the door.

Suddenly I tripped. Sprawled on the ground, I scrambled for a toe-hold in the dirt. My heart pounded till I thought it would explode. I was halfway to my feet when I saw my brothers frantically motioning me to get up.

I sprang upright without looking back. One more scream, and my legs were pumping as fast as they could. My shoes barely touched the ground. I dashed across the yard, through the hedge, and down the block. Faster and faster I ran.

It wasn't until I burst through the screen door into my house, slammed it, and slumped to the carpet that I noticed my brothers standing around. Tears of fright were streaming down my face.

"The bogeyman almost got you!" Paul said. The others nodded solemnly, and then Paul said something about me wetting my pants. I looked down and for the first time noticed that both legs were soaked. My brothers started laughing, and I burst into a fresh round of tears.

Suddenly Paul was on his knees with his hand on my shoulder. "It's OK, Susie. It wasn't really the bogeyman. Everything will be fine. Please stop crying. It wasn't the bogeyman."

I peered at him through waterlogged eyes, lost about what he was saying and why they were laughing.

"Look, it was just a stupid joke," he said. "It wasn't the bogeyman—just ol' Jake disguised in his catcher's gear. Please stop crying now. It was a dumb thing to do. Please stop. It wasn't the bogeyman. . . ."

When my brothers got to be too much for me, I simply drew away by myself with my imaginary playmate, a black stallion named Boo. Together, Boo and I would disappear behind the big, green easy chair in the living room, where I pretended we were camped out in the mountains.

We'd lie low around a blazing fire, eating make-believe pancakes, and then we'd bed down with my head on his hide as the pretend coals turned to little orange stars. In my mind, Boo and I went everywhere: to the ocean where we galloped at dusk in the foamy surf; to hidden valleys where we'd rob from the rich and give to the poor; even to the moon. Everywhere we went, we ate our pancakes.

As with most kids, there were a couple of times when I wanted to run away from home. And so I'd wrap my red-and-white checkered scarf around a pile of precious belongings, knot it to a stick, and then disappear with Boo behind the living room chair. It was a barrier, like a giant boulder or a mountain's face, which shielded me from rain, sleet, snow, or the troubles of childhood.

"I've finally had it," I would announce to anybody within earshot. "I'm running away."

"Be home by dinner," Mom would say before I turned to go.

"We've got our grub. Boo and I will eat pancakes."

"Well, come back for dessert then."

"Maybe," I'd say. And then I'd duck behind the chair. In a moment I'd be racing away with Boo at a fast gallop, rushing down hills and across plains, feeling the wind lick at my face, and sensing, once again, that life was everything it should be for a little deaf girl of five.

4

A PERSONAL ANTHEM

P erhaps because of the absence of sound in my life, smells were as vivid to me as colors. The deep, musky smell of our fireplace was coffee brown; the pungent coal-burning furnace, black as ebony; the fresh aroma after a summer rain, yellow as butter-colored marigolds; the scent of freshly mowed lawns, peacock blue. But nothing compared to the sweet pink scent of Mom's freshly baked pies, cookies, cakes, and bread or the familiar greenish smell of paint and turpentine that was as much a part of my father as his love.

I waited for my father every night on the driveway, and when he pulled up at four thirty, he always greeted me with a hug and a smile as big as the horizon. I'd grab his lunch box and he'd grab me, setting me up on his shoulders as he walked into the house.

Just inside the threshold, he'd kiss Mom and then go change his white, paint-splattered bib overalls, wash out his brushes and rollers, and scrub his hands for five straight minutes as if he were a surgeon preparing for the operating room.

Except for Saturdays, meals were a formal, sit-down, meat-and-potatoes affair that began a half hour after Dad arrived home from work. It was a regimen you could set your watch by. At exactly five o'clock, he'd take the head seat at our cherry dining table, shake the military creases from his napkin, and spread it in his lap. He often said he could shave with the straight edge of one of the napkins, and Mom would flash a smile. She starched and ironed everything, including our underwear.

Though Dad was only five-foot-eight, he seemed much taller because he was rail thin, due in part to having contracted spinal meningitis in his youth. The disease didn't effect his refined, sculpted looks, however, and when he wore his dark suit, he looked as distinguished as the minister of the Cornersburg Methodist Church, which we attended weekly.

I think my family went to church primarily because that's what good people were supposed to do in Boardman, Ohio, in the 1950s. I don't know how attending church every Sunday effected others in my family, but I got nothing out of it. I couldn't hear the songs or the prayers or the little lessons the teachers taught. I went because I had to.

Nevertheless, I can't remember a time when I didn't believe in God. Mom taught me about Jesus' love—that he would always help me, no matter what. When my dog wasn't around to hold or share my feelings with, I talked with Jesus. I'd tell him I was lonely and that there were things I didn't understand about my silent world and the way people treated me. In his own time he would somehow make everything better, I knew—and perhaps even turn my ears back on.

Hanging on the side wall of my bedroom was a picture of Jesus, given me by one of Mom's bridge partners. Aunt Jenny, I called her. A heavy but radiant woman, she laughed easily and was always full of love. She often brought me presents when she came over, but I liked the Jesus picture best.

I stared at the picture when I felt alone and small. In the picture, Jesus wore a flowing white robe like my mother's. His was a kind, bearded face, with brown shoulder-length hair. He stood outside a house, knocking on the door. That door remained shut because nobody heard the knocks. I wondered if the people who lived there were deaf like myself. But Jesus didn't seem impatient. By the look on his face, it seemed he would just keep on knocking and knocking and knocking.

After receiving that picture, I always kept my bedroom door open. I could get all the privacy I needed simply by shutting my eyes. If I really wanted to be alone, I went outside or sought refuge with Boo behind the wing chair in the living room or under the dining room table. But I never closed my door. I didn't want to keep Jesus standing outside, knocking and waiting for me to ask him in.

After church we all trooped home to a big dinner. All the household chores and gardening were completed by Saturday, allowing Sundays to be reserved for rest— or pursuing Dad's great love of baseball.

Once offered a contract as a minor league baseball player, he chose instead to work as a commercial artist, painting posters for the area movie theaters. Having the Depression to contend with, he needed a sure and steady job. Playing ball seemed too frivolous for the times, and he even quit high school to begin working, as did Mom. When he discovered he could make more money painting houses than movie posters, he made the switch. But the love of baseball never left his blood, and from him I learned how to throw fast, swing hard, and slide quick. I could catch anything he hit and spent many Sunday afternoons with him shagging flies and snagging grounders.

With three brothers, a neighborhood of boys, and a baseball-loving dad, I never had much time for dolls. Mom tried to encourage more feminine behavior by teaching me to bake and sending me to charm school. But when Dad pulled out the mitts, I forgot everything about etiquette, scrambled for the door, and left the dolls to have a tea party by themselves. The best time of day was ball time!

As the summer gave way to fall, I was a bundle of excitement as I anticipated the start of kindergarten. For years, school was among the things that separated me from my brothers. They could play outside after dark and stay up late at night. And then in the morning, they got on the school bus, leaving me behind: the baby with her mother.

The night before my first day of kindergarten, I took a long bubble bath, scrubbing and scraping away the remnants of summer that lingered behind my ears and clung to the bony places of my knees and elbows. Then Mom laid out on my bed my green-and-red plaid dress, fresh underwear, socks, and red Buster Brown shoes.

That first day I awoke with the sun, feeling like I was going to a parade. Mom drove me to school for the afternoon session, took a picture of me with the teacher, and then disappeared until pick-up time at three o'clock.

Sunlight gushed through the bank of windows, filling the classroom with brightness and happiness. Big colorful flowers decorated the wall, and shelves were stocked like a toy store. The afternoon began with one of the boys wetting his pants. After he was cleaned up, the teacher, Mrs. Hatcher, sat down at the piano and played songs I couldn't hear.

Kindergarten was a special time of life because it opened my world to others my age. In their company, I felt I was a normal little girl, no different from anybody else. They didn't care that I talked funny or couldn't learn the Pledge of Allegiance or sing songs that everybody else knew. I could play and run and swing and finger paint just like the others, and that's all that seemed to matter.

I enjoyed their innocence while it lasted. Little did I realize how soon it would disappear and the children would grow up to become far less tolerant and forgiving.

With the advent of autumn, our backyard baseball diamond was transformed into a football field, and the greenery all about us changed to a palette of flaming yellows and oranges and reds. My father raked the fallen leaves into heaping piles that my brothers loaded into large drop cloths and dragged into a master pile, which I'd burrow through until they shooed me out and set it afire.

With the trees bare of leaves, I saw birds that I otherwise never noticed. Because I never heard their chirps and chatters, I never thought to look for them in the branches at other times of the year. Likewise, I seldom noticed planes in the sky because I was oblivious to their distant roar. My eyes kept busy enough at ground level with the silent onrush of speeding cars, darting children, and other roadside hazards. It always took my father to nudge me, point skyward, and say, "Look, the ducks are flying south."

Upon spotting the giant V of flapping birds, I broke into a million-watt smile and pointed out the migration to my brothers. "The birdies! The birdies!" I squealed, as if I'd just discovered some profound secret of the universe. When they ignored me, I realized I'd spotted something that was apparently special only to me. Because the birds were seen by them every day, they were never really seen at all.

I never grew tired of the wonders around me, and I especially enjoyed the cooling season. To me, fall meant seeing my breath in the morning, frost-covered lawns, carving pumpkins, chilly nights, hot cider, and backyard bonfires.

At the close of an autumn day, I loved nothing more than to crawl in bed with my parents and snuggle between them. On cold nights Mom wore both a nightgown and robe to bed. And in the morning she draped her robe around me so I felt warm and protected, and then she fixed my favorite hot breakfast.

Fall was also football season. As the youngest child, I was always carried along to the high school stadium on Friday night to watch Paul march in the band or witness Billy chase other players around the field.

Billy, who was thirteen years older than I, was a lanky six-footer who could kick a football or slam a baseball clear to the moon. Because of our age difference, he was like a second father to me. He gave me baths, showed me picture books, let me climb on his shoulders, and otherwise be a pesky little sister.

I loved to watch Billy play football, but I mostly liked to see him laugh, even though I never heard him. At first his eyes would squint, and he'd bust out with a smile as big as the outdoors. Then a little shake would start to build from somewhere down in his toes and work its way up until he was shaking and laughing so hard that his face turned beet red and his eyes flooded with tears.

I don't remember when I first noticed the family troubles, but I'll never forget when, at age five, my mother approached me as I brushed my teeth early one morning. For days there had been tension in the air. Everybody in the family walked around, purposefully staying out of each other's way and avoiding even eye contact.

As far as I knew, nobody was yelling at each other, but I could see they were screaming on the inside. Faces were etched with frowns and pained eyes, and bodies were stooped by the burden of unseen pressures. Words were exchanged like bullets, and everybody performed gymnastics to avoid being in the same room together. Our house felt like a volcano, and I just tried to keep out of the way of the pending eruption.

As I stood there with the toothbrush in my mouth that one morning so long ago, I felt Mom's hand on my shoulder. Turning to face her, I saw stress written on her face.

"There's something I want to tell you," she said. It was obvious she meant business, and I read her lips as carefully as I could. "Billy doesn't love us anymore. He ran away from home, and we won't be seeing him anymore."

"Billy *what?*" I said, unsure I'd gotten it right.

"Billy's gone—ran away. He doesn't love us anymore."

Her eyes were red, as if she'd been crying for days. And then her eyes suddenly filled with more tears. She tried to hold back, but when she left the bathroom, I saw her small shoulders shaking.

I followed her into her bedroom and into the middle of a fight with my father. Their words and angry looks slammed back and forth with blitzkrieg force. The two of them darted back and forth around the bed, their arms stabbing the air to make a point. But when they saw me, they purposefully turned their heads so I couldn't see their words.

That's all I was told: Billy was gone and didn't love us anymore. I felt like I'd been hit by a truck. I ran to my room and quickly got dressed. I knew that if Billy's things were still in his dresser, he'd be back.

Dashing up the stairs and into his room, which he shared with my two other brothers, I threw open all his drawers. They were empty, except for one pair of socks. I held them to my chest, and through my tears I stared at his graduation picture on the dresser. It was true. Billy was gone.

I stumbled downstairs and out into the backyard where we played football. Then I got down on my knees in the wet grass. "Dear Jesus, I know you can work all this out," I cried toward heaven as tears burned my cheeks. "I know you'll bring Billy home. I don't know how, but you will. Please, Jesus. I'll wait because I know you'll do it. Please, Jesus. Please."

The hardest thing for me was wondering what I'd done to make Billy run away. I thought it was my fault.

He was like a second father to me, and I couldn't imagine why he didn't love me. I couldn't figure it out.

All I knew was what I saw, and in those months I saw much but heard nothing. I saw the tears, the anger. But I never heard the fights or the muffled, behind-closed-doors disputes that prompted whatever was going bad with our family. I saw Mom storm into her bedroom with increasing regularity and refuse to come out—not even getting out of bed—for days at a time.

I would snuggle up close to her, whispering in her ear that I would do anything to make her happy again. But when that didn't help, I talked it over with Jesus, or took a ride with Boo behind the green chair, and otherwise waited out the storm. Not knowing what was going on, I asked God to make things better.

My parents were generally very loving toward each other and the children. I never doubted their love, either for myself or for each other. How well I remembered the many times Dad would walk through the door, pull Mom suddenly into his arms, and then take off jitterbugging across the room! Even during this time, my father tried to console Mom. He hovered over her, encouraging her to come out of the bedroom. When his efforts failed, he withdrew into a quiet shell, looking more worn and defeated than I'd ever seen him before.

During these bedroom days, Dad made the dinners, and we ate with Mom's empty plate at the table. I'd see her curled up in bed, still in her nightgown, her hair a mess and her skin looking pale and stretched. In the morning, Dad made sure I was dressed and neat, doing his best to keep the family going.

When Mom finally came out, she pulled me aside and told me that Billy had gotten married.

"Billy? Married?"

"He's bringing Barbara over next week to meet the family, along with her parents."

"Barbara?"

"His wife."

I ran down the hall, jumping up and down, knowing my backyard prayers had been answered. Billy was coming home!

I stood by the window each day, waiting. My anticipation grew till I thought I would explode. When the day of their visit arrived, her parents showed up first. It was awkward because nobody took their coats. They just stood there inside the front door, looking like they were ready to leave.

Finally, Mom pointed to the sofa and they sat down. Dad, sitting in the green easy chair, mostly just stared at his feet. The man kept adjusting his tie and running his fingers along the crease in his suit pants. His wife watched the clock.

"They should never have married," Mom blurted suddenly. Everybody looked up. "Barbara is Catholic."

"Just a second here," the man began, his eyebrows arched like the wings of a hawk.

"I'm sorry, but that's my ways. We're a Protestant family, and Billy shouldn't have married a Catholic. That spells trouble."

"It's the Protestants what's trouble," the man responded. He glanced at his wife, but she looked too upset for words.

I turned away and glued my face to the window, waiting, praying desperately that Billy would show up soon.

When I turned back around, Barbara's parents were on their feet. My heart ached. On the inside I screamed, "No, don't go! They'll come! Please, I know they're coming!" But they left, and Billy never showed up.

I ran into my room and threw myself on the bed. I didn't understand why Jesus didn't bring Billy home. I had no idea where he lived. He just disappeared from my life, and I didn't know where to find him. Nor did I know it would be twenty long, silent years before he would come home again.

After crying that night until my body ached and tears could no longer flow, I squeezed my eyes shut and took a long, slow, deep breath. And then I began to sing:

> *Si-i-lent night, ho-o-ly night*
> *All-l-l is calm, all-l-l is bright. . . .*

Things were neither calm nor bright, but singing the words made it seem so. I'd learned the lyrics and music in my mother's lap, curled up with her in the rocking chair in happier days. The sun was often low in the sky, either in the morning or evening, and the rays of light would slant through the window and across the carpet, catching little specks of fairy dust in their beam. As I sat there watching her lips sing, the sun sometimes caught her hair in just the right way that it glowed like the hair of angels.

We spent hours together in the weathered old chair, rocking back and forth as she mouthed the words. I would lay my head against her chest to feel the rise and fall of each breath and place my hand on her throat to pick up the vibrations. My eyes and hands became my ears, and slowly I was able to sing along with her, smiling when she smiled her approval back at me.

Of all the songs I learned, "Silent Night" was my favorite. Sung in December by most people, it became my personal anthem that I belted out anywhere, anytime, even in the middle of the year.

"The words will comfort you," my mother told me early on. And so they did, especially on long, lonely nights such as when Billy left home. I sang it almost like a prayer, the words soothing the depths of my soul.

It never crossed my mind that others could hear me. But years later, my parents said they sometimes cried to hear me belt out those words at the top of my lungs following a great hurt or disappointment. Mom said they'd be just about ready to come into my bedroom to say, "It's OK; don't cry," when suddenly my sobs would stop and the words of "Silent Night" would drift from beneath my bedroom door.

5

SOARING

Midway through my kindergarten year on a crisp Saturday morning, our family piled into the car and headed for the Boardman roller skating rink. It was a treat my parents allowed my brothers on weekends—if they'd done their chores, eaten their vegetables, and been nice to me.

As I watched Paul and Bobby lace up their skates, I longed for the time when I'd be old enough to join them. I knew that day would eventually come, but I thought the wait would kill me. My jealous eyes followed them as they tugged the laces tight around their ankles, and then slipped out onto the oval and whizzed off at breakneck speed.

As we were preparing to leave, the rink instructor, Johnny Sauers, approached my parents. He was tall and blond, with muscles everywhere. They talked for a while, and then Johnny turned around and nodded toward me. My father glanced over. I saw him shake his head no.

". . . too young," he said, which was all I caught. My eyes jumped to Johnny's lips.

"You ought to give it a try—at least see what she can do," he said, smiling easily.

My father looked down, studying his shoes. Then he turned his eyes back on me for a long moment. Our

eyes caught. The corner of his mouth turned up, and I
saw him wink.

Five minutes later, I was laced into a pair of skates and
in the middle of the rink, holding onto Johnny's hand
for dear life. He led me through the maze of jumping,
spinning, kamikaze skaters. Then he slipped his hand
from mine, skated backward a few yards, and motioned
for me to come to him. I made it without falling. He moved
farther away, and again I stayed on my feet. Before long
I was skating back and forth through the center of the rink.

"I think she's a natural," Johnny beamed to my parents as we came off the oval. "With a few lessons, she'd
be something."

My father looked over at Mom, who was smiling.
Then he glanced at me and nodded his consent. "We'll
give it a try," he said.

Translated, that meant weekly lessons on Saturday
mornings, followed by practice Saturday afternoon,
Sunday night, and twice a week after school. My parents didn't believe in half effort. If I was going to skate,
they wanted me to be the best.

Within a few weeks I was skating backward, and not
long thereafter I was doing waltz jumps and shoot-the-
duck tucks—a move in which one leg is extended while
the other is tucked under the body. Observing my rapid
progress, Johnny suggested that I enter local competitions, and my parents readily agreed.

After choreographing a simple routine, Johnny had
his work cut out for him. Every jump, landing, spin,
and movement had to be flawlessly synchronized to
the beat of the music. That's hard enough for most skaters; it's much harder when you can't hear the music!

Taking my hand in his, Johnny skated the routine with me again and again to perfect my speed and timing. After weeks of side-by-side practice, he finally let me try it solo. From the far end of the rink, he signalled when the song began. I then launched my routine, following his lead as he marked each beat with his waving hand like a bandmaster. If I fell or hesitated at any point, I was lost.

That's invariably what happened. Midway through the routine, again and again, Johnny skated onto the rink, waved me off, and said I wasn't with the music. I felt like I did with Miss Vetterle in front of the mirror. He was more demanding than he had a right to be, and I felt like a failure. I would never get it right. But after endless hours of practice, as I should have known, the routine became as natural to me as breathing.

My very first competition was at age five in the diaper division. The song I skated to that everybody but me heard was Patti Page's "The Mama Doll Song," with backup by Jack Rael and his orchestra:

> *I once had a doll that was all dressed in
>   white,*
> *I called her my baby, and I'd hold her tight.*
> *Her eyes were so blue and her cheeks were
>   so red,*
> *But I loved her most of all each time she said:*
> *"Mama, Mama, Mama, Mama"—one little
>   word she knew,*
> *"Mama, Mama, Mama, Mama"—to me it
>   meant, "I love you."*

I wore a white dress, which Mom had covered with sequins, and carried a little doll with an identical handmade costume and tiny matching skates. I rocked the doll to the beat of Johnny's waving hand, laid it down asleep in the middle of the rink as I launched my routine of spins and jumps, and then returned to the doll and finished together.

I smiled so much my face hurt afterward. And though I didn't win first place on my first outing, the thrill of competition and seeing the crowd's applause made a lasting impact on me that fueled the lonely, often painful hours of practice that eventually led to the state championship.

My father took extra jobs to pay for the skating lessons, which quickly expanded into tap dance and music lessons. My parents were dead serious about their early vow to make me as much a part of the hearing world as possible, even though I never heard the *rat-ta-tat* rhythm of my taps or a single, solitary note of music I ever played.

On my sixth birthday, a truck pulled up to the house and men with hairy faces unloaded a big piano. My parents were all smiles when it was delivered, but I was not impressed. As far as I could tell, the thing was useless. It took up a lot of space in the living room, and the black and white keys did nothing when I pushed on them.

However, Mom said no child, not even a deaf one, should grow up without learning the piano. So I spent large chunks of my afternoon sitting on a bench in front of that upright, pushing the keys in a particular order. The rule of the house was that I could do nothing after school until I had practiced at least a half hour. Later, the time increased to an hour or more. It was a grand waste of time, as far as I could tell, and I fought Mom before and during most practice sessions. She always won.

I figured her basic job, as she sat next to me at the piano, was to lift my hands off the keyboard and shake her head every time I pushed a wrong key. Mine was to push the right keys, which I seldom did in the early years.

"Do it again," she'd say, and I would stare hard at the sheet music and try to match the notes with their corresponding keys. Moments later, she would again lift my fingers free. "Don't bang. Try again."

After the third or fourth repetition, I felt my heart beating in my head. "I can't do this anymore," I announced.

"Yes you can."

"This is stupid."

"Start again."

"I'm tired."

"Do you want to go to your room after practice?"

"I'll go now," I said, squirming down from the bench.

"Susan Kay, get back up here! Now!"

"I'm going to my room!" I said, backing away fast and then turning to run.

She was always faster, and caught me by the shirt collar before I was five steps away.

"Sit down, young lady!" she said, dragging me back to the bench.

"No!"

"Now, or you'll get the swatter!"

I grudgingly climbed back onto the bench. Then I slammed my fists into the keys as fast and hard as I could. Mom's fingers dug into my shoulders. Wrenching away, I reached out and knocked the music to the floor. She immediately had me by the arm as her face turned red and squashed up into a mask.

"Pick up that music and get back up here! Now! Let's move! And don't you dare throw another tantrum, young lady! One more outburst and you'll be here all day. Understand?"

I glared at her.

"Do you understand?"

Gritting my teeth, I forced my head to move a fraction of an inch.

"Is that yes?"

This time I nodded until I thought I'd shake my head off.

"Hands on the keyboard!"

"Do I have to?"

"Hands up or you'll be very, very, very sorry," she said and then looked away. When she looked back, her eyes were teary. After a long silence, she finally said, "You fight and fight and fight." And then she added her standard refrain, "Someday . . . yes, *someday* you'll thank me."

When it came to discipline at home, Dad never laid a hand on me. If I did something wrong, he merely looked at me and I fell apart. Mom, on the other hand, administered justice with a lime green fly swatter that was as big as Kansas.

One memorable confrontation occurred when I was playing across the street and my friends said Mom was calling me for dinner. I knew she wouldn't accept the excuse that I didn't hear her because my brothers or friends always relayed her beckon. But on that one occasion I just kept playing, only to suddenly look up some time later and see her heading toward me with a glint in her hazel eyes and that dreaded fly swatter in her hand.

I took off running in the general direction of home, but along a route that was out of her reach. My legs moved as fast as they could, but when I glanced back, she was gaining on me. Darting down a grassy slope, I went to jump a small ditch beside the road but landed wrong and tumbled backward into a foot of slime. Mom grabbed me out by the collar and then lashed at my bare legs with the swatter. I got it three times—for not coming when she called, for running from her, and for mucking up my clothes. Then she gave me a fourth stinging wallop—just for good measure.

Another confrontation occurred when I got up early one day from my piano practice. Mom dragged me back to the bench, but as soon as she turned the corner I was off and running. I got as far as the dining room when she blazed through the doorway with the swatter cocked above her head. I flew around the dining table, and she gave pursuit. After a couple of laps, I fell to the floor and started laughing. Then Mom started laughing. I figured I was safe at that point, but before I knew what was happening, she was at my side, and I was screaming bloody murder as the swatter found its target on the fleshy part of my legs.

Mom arranged for private piano lessons for me throughout elementary school and served as my ears during practice sessions. She was convinced I would someday be thankful. Eventually I *was*—thankful I never heard a single mistake I made!

Together we worked through early beginner books, playing "Three Blind Mice" and duets such as "Heart and Soul" and "Chopsticks." Years later, once I could understand and distinguish the vibrations of music, I started playing classical music. The more violent the song, the better I liked it. I particularly enjoyed Beethoven, whose symphonies and sonatas became increasingly violent when he lost his hearing. Consequently, the vibrations were stronger, and I was better able to feel the beat.

Music, like a heartbeat, would become the pulse of my life. It conveyed the essence of my feelings. If I was happy, I played marches, peppy tunes by Rodgers and Hammerstein, and boogie-woogie. When angry, I pounded out sonatas and sonatinas, or pieces such as Grieg's Concerto in A Minor that start out with a *bam!*

An emotional outlet for both joy and despair, music also became my prayer. When my mood grew dark and lonely, and my conversations with God seemed to bounce off the ceiling, I pounded hymns on the keyboard with all my might. Somehow I think God understood. I'm just grateful I didn't hear what it sounded like!

As my skating lessons also progressed, I was aware that the other kids taking lessons all had their own skates. They weren't just any skates. They were Douglas Snyder

Deluxe models. They flashed with raw power as they jetted by, while I felt like a bad accident in my thirty-five-cent rentals. I tried not to notice, but how could I not notice such beautiful creatures that were so lean and smooth and fast? I might as well have not noticed I was deaf.

The young boys and girls, laced and tall in their Douglas Snyders, were a blur of speed as they raced around and around the wooden oval. When they passed, they kicked up turbulence that slapped my face like the trailing blast of a highway truck. And when they jumped, they launched airborne as if rockets were strapped to their feet.

I glanced down at my rental skates. They were dead and tired and as heavy as the stump of an old, weathered oak. In them, my feet could hardly move. I tried to jump, but I was mired in concrete.

"Dad, I want my own skates," I said one afternoon after a lesson.

"There's plenty for rent right here at the rink," he replied, hardly bothering to turn around so I could read his lips.

"But they're not Douglas Snyders."

"What difference does that make?"

I wondered if he'd lost his head. What *difference* did it make? The difference was like night and day! I could either soar like an eagle, or remain caged like a pet store parakeet. He might as well have asked what difference it made to have gas in the car. But how could I explain any of that to him?

"They're just . . . oh, it's how they *feel* and the way they *look*," I said, staring at the rental boots that were worn and wobbly and as wrinkled as a bulldog's face. Maybe at one time they had support and grace and speed, but all that had long since disappeared. In them I couldn't race the wind or jump houses and trees. They didn't even have toe stops. "Could I, Dad? Please?" I tried again.

"Well . . . ," he said, bending to help me unlace the skates, which was as good as saying no. I knew he didn't understand a word I said or thought or felt. And no wonder: All the kid in him had grown up.

Several months passed, and it was all I could do to hide my frustration. How could I possibly compete with other skaters, who could stop on a dime with their adjustable toe stops, who had missiles on their feet while I wore lead weights? At night, I dreamed of eagles soaring, soaring, soaring with the wind.

And then one Saturday after practice, an amazing thing happened. Dad took me up to the counter at the skating rink, and the manager pulled two boxes off a shelf. He handed them to my father, and they exchanged smiles. The manager then came around to our side and sat me down on a nearby bench. He took off my old rental skates and then opened the larger of the two boxes.

I thought my heart would burst. Inside was a pair of new boots. Douglas Snyder Deluxe models! As I stared at the stiff white leather uppers and miles of white laces, I felt a wind suddenly stir. And when I cautiously reached out to touch the boots, the wind gusted up as if a whole flock of eagles was whipping around and around the rink.

The manager, his eyes all atwinkle, pulled the boots from the box and slipped them onto my feet. He adjusted the tongues and laces, and had me flex my toes and lean sideways to test the ankle support. His mouth hung slightly open as he worked, and I wondered if he noticed the Fourth of July feelings that flashed and sparkled and exploded inside my feet just inches from his face.

When he finished, he rolled back on his heels and gave a nod to my father. I glanced over, and when our eyes met we exchanged a deep and profound silence. The boots were a perfect fit.

The manager then opened the other box, explaining that he needed to bolt the boots to the plates inside and mount the wheels. I leaned forward and peered over the lip of the box. Eight wooden wheels, dark and polished, rested inside like Easter eggs. Beside them were the gleaming metal plates, as shiny as the bumper of a new car.

"Today?" I asked.

"A week," he said. "Give me till next Saturday."

I waited and waited. The next seven days dragged on like months. The dawn of each new morning brought the hope of spring as I raced to ask if it was Saturday yet. But when Mom shook her head, my expectancy withered, and the rest of the morning stretched on like the long, hot, boring weeks of summer. My resolve wilted through the afternoon as if pummeled by the blustery winds of autumn, and the period between dinner and bedtime was like waiting for the chill of winter to pass.

Finally, one morning, Mom didn't shake her head. Saturday had arrived. I ran to her, gave her a big squeeze, and darted outside to wait by the car until it was time to leave for the rink. When we arrived, I sprinted up to the counter. The manager had evidently seen me coming because he had my skates—my wonderful and incomparable Douglas Snyders—waiting right there at eye level, lined up toe to toe. I snatched them up and, hugging them tightly to my chest, slipped off into a corner where I could be all by myself, alone with my skates.

I put my nose against the snow white leather, inhaled deep and long, and then held my breath until I thought I would die and go to heaven. I wished I could have captured that warm, familiar, fast smell and canned it for sale. But I couldn't wait and sit there thinking of things like that. The rink was beckoning. Quick as a flash, I laced up my Douglas Snyders and raced for the skating oval.

Suddenly I became a bird in flight, soaring on wings like an eagle and cutting against the wind. My flight was fast and smooth, and my hair whipped my face as if I were holding my head outside the window of a speeding car. Faster and faster and faster I flew, leaving other skaters in my turbulent wake. Then I jumped, reaching a height I'd never before experienced.

Free from gravity, I hung weightless in the air, frozen in time. And not until the very moment when I thought I would hit my head on the roof did I float back to earth. Several minutes later when I touched down, I realized for the first time there were coils of springs inside my skates—my powerful, gravity-defying, spring-loaded Douglas Snyder Deluxe skates!

6

DAZE OF MY LIFE

ithin the shelter of my family and neighborhood friends, my deafness remained a small thing—in the sense that a slight tear in a feather pillow is a small thing. With gentle handling and love, I did fine. But when I graduated into the rough-and-tumble world of early elementary school, small differences among children were magnified. They fingered and poked at that slight tear, enlarging it as they tugged on any loose thread along the seam.

The poking began the first day of first grade when the teacher asked the students to stand and introduce themselves. I thought nothing of it. But when I smiled and said, "My name is Susan," everybody laughed. I didn't know what they were laughing about, but I soon realized they laughed every time I spoke. At roll call, on the playground, in the reading circle—if I opened my mouth, their shoulders shook and their mouths twisted up into devilish grins.

By the following year, I was terrified to read aloud in small groups. My second-grade teacher, Mrs. Miller, was a tall, slender Miss America look-alike. As she worked her way around the circle, asking students to read, my heart raced. The closer she drew to me, the more my face burned and my stomach knotted.

When she finally called my name, I didn't know where we were. She pointed her red fingernail at the line "See Spot run," and I struggled to pronounce the words as if lifting a heavy barbell off my chest.

"Thhh . . . thhh . . . thheee . . . Thhh . . . Thhhbod . . . rrrr . . . uuuu . . . rruuunn . . . ," I began, feeling the horrible, lifeless weight of my tongue in my mouth. It felt like it was nailed to my wooden lips. As I sweated out each letter, nothing in my mouth worked right. When I felt I was making headway, I glanced up for encouragement, only to see ten faces laughing at me around the circle.

I tried to make my lips utter the words the laughing children found so easy. Somebody elbowed me, and I looked up again with my face burning. Shoulders were shaking everywhere. I couldn't continue. And then I *wouldn't* continue. Squeezing back the tears, I refused to read.

From that point on, whenever the teacher asked me a question in class, I felt dizzy and nauseous. I sat in the front row so I could read her lips, but I knew people would laugh if I answered the question. Sometimes I wanted to ask a question myself, but thought maybe somebody behind me had already asked it. So I just sat there and didn't say anything. If I didn't speak, nobody laughed.

When the class moved on to spelling, Mrs. Miller would say a word, and I did my best to read her lips and write down what I thought I saw. But without the context of a sentence, I didn't have enough clues to work with. And if I missed the opening lip movement, the word *book* looked almost identical to *look* or *took* or *cook* or dozens of other words. Other kids' papers came back with bright stars and smiling faces on them. Mine were covered with red check marks.

Shortly thereafter, Mrs. Miller had a conference with Mom. I didn't know what they said, but I knew my teacher was talking about me because I saw tears in Mom's eyes. We returned home with a list of spelling words, and after dinner Mom sat me down at the table. She said a word and I repeated it back to her. She shook her head, and I tried another word. I fought her every step of the way as the horrible, familiar feelings from school churned in my stomach.

When I finally pushed back from the table, Mom placed her hand over mine. "You must try," she said. "You must keep working and not give up. You can do it. You *have* to do it."

The following week Mom volunteered to be room mother, and Dad presented me with my own copy of Webster's dictionary, just like my brothers had. It was thick and heavy and blue and filled with pages of words—words such as *automobile* and *fudge* and *worm.* With it on my dresser I felt grown up and smart. But when I stumbled over the simplest words in class, I tucked the dictionary in the darkest corner of my bottom drawer.

My troubles intensified when two boys in Mrs. Miller's class appointed themselves as my guardian demons, following as close as my shadow wherever I went. Stalking me like a wounded animal, they and their friends hounded me and made my life miserable.

Raymond was squat and dark-skinned, with hair cropped close to his head. Jimmy had the distinguished looks of a junior IBM executive. Every hair on his head remained perfectly combed throughout the day, and his glasses never slipped down the bridge of his nose. Uniquely blessed with good looks, he was also uniquely cursed with heartless cruelty.

At recess they lingered by the drinking fountain or bathrooms, waiting for me to come outside. Then they cornered me, shoved me around, made faces at me, and ridiculed my looks and speech.

"Lookie, lookie, here cometh Thuthie," they said, exaggerating a lisp I could see. Then one of them slipped behind me and kicked me in the rump.

"Deaf as a doornail and dumb as a dog!" they said. I whipped around and felt the other yank my pigtail.

"Baby Thuthie can't talk," they said.

"Baby Thuthie want a bottle?" they said.

Waves of torment washed over me as they mimicked the way I sounded to them. Another foot smashed into my behind, and suddenly I could take no more. What they didn't know is that I had three big brothers. I'd been taught to fight.

I rushed at them like an angered grizzly bear, baring my teeth and lashing out with all the fury I could muster. I was fighting for survival, so I fought hard. We tumbled to the ground in a heap, kicking and biting and scratching. I stopped only when the rough hand of the playground supervisor yanked me up and dragged us all off to the principal's.

At the office Raymond and Jimmy were summoned first, and I was left to fume and stew in the reception area. When they departed, they thumbed their noses at me and laughed. Then the secretary ushered me in and sat me in a hard chair across from the cold gray desk of the principal. He was stocky and muscular and dressed in a wrinkled suit. He stared at me, as if seeing who would blink first. Then he adjusted his tie and asked why I had hit Jimmy and Raymond.

"Why?" I responded, not knowing if I'd read his lips correctly. *Why would he ask me why? Wasn't that obvious?*

"Yes, why did you hit them?"

"Because . . . well, because they were making fun of me and pushing me and pulling my hair and—"

"You cannot go through life fighting and causing trouble," he said.

"They were—"

"You need to apologize to both boys."

I looked at him blankly, not understanding what he said.

"To tell them you're sorry."

"Sorry?" I asked, my mind racing. I turned and stared outside his window. I saw the sprawling lawn and newly planted maple trees in front of the school, and in the distance, the roofs of homes and a church under construction. "Sorry?" I repeated.

"Yes."

I shook my head. "But they were making fun of me, and I—"

"Two wrongs don't make a right. You still need to say you are sorry."

"You don't understand. They started it."

"I don't care who started it, young lady."

"But they—"

"No excuses. You were very, very bad—so bad that you must be disciplined. I must spank you."

"Spank?"

He nodded, then stood up and reached behind the desk for a large wooden paddle. When I saw what he had in mind, my heart broke and I began to cry for the first time. Huge tears rolled down my cheeks and fell into my lap.

"Why do I . . . have to get . . . spanked . . . for them making . . . making fun of me?" I pleaded through my tears.

"You were a bad girl."

"I don't . . . understand . . . why I had . . . to be made fun of . . . and then . . . get spanked . . . too," I said, sobbing harder.

The principal looked at me stiffly, impassively. And then he walked around to my chair, motioned for me to stand up, and led me to the side of his desk. There he made me bend over toward the wall and gave me a single, hard, solid, stinging, humiliating swat—on the very spot where the boys had kicked me.

I was more infuriated than hurt by the spanking. For the life of me, I couldn't understand why the principal paddled me. Was I wrong to stand up to those who tormented, humiliated, and laughed at me? Was I wrong for fighting back when they cornered and kicked and made fun of me? Nor did I understand why the boys used me as a target. Their twisted, laughing faces confused me. Why did they pick on me? Had I done or said something bad? Had I mistreated them? I looked normal and dressed like everybody else. So why?

What I wanted more than anything was to be understood. I wanted someone other than my parents to draw alongside me and say they loved me and hated the awful treatment I received from my tormentors. I wanted the teacher to stand up and tell the class how I'd learned to speak and read lips and tap-dance and play the piano and roller-skate. I wanted the principal to quit spanking me every time I was sent to his office.

But that was all fantasy—just like my dream at night that Raymond and Jimmy would approach me one day and say they were sorry and invite me to play together on the playground. Such dreams were not to come true.

Skating enabled me to escape into my own little world, where I was isolated from the ridicule, laughter, and alienation I experienced in the classroom. Feeling totally frustrated in school, I found release at the rink, where I could jump as high and skate as fast as I could. It was the place where I regularly found freedom, a corner of the world where I could just be me.

At the rink, my skating instructor, Johnny, introduced me to an Italian boy with wavy, charcoal-black hair who was my same height and just a few months older. His name was Mickey Nuzzo, and he became my skating partner for the next few years.

Whether in practice or in competition, Mickey and I always dressed alike. Our moms kept in touch, and if I wore a navy blue skirt with a blouse, Mickey arrived in matching navy pants and a shirt.

In pairs competition, poise was everything. We stood perfectly erect, chins up, fingers together, eyes focused on a certain spot on the wall, forever smiling.

When the music started, Mickey was supposed to gently squeeze my hand. If he was mad or just wanted to reinforce that I was a girl and he was a boy, he squeezed and didn't stop squeezing until my hand turned red and I yelped at him through my forced smile. As we picked up speed, I pinched his side until he loosened his grip.

The audience never suspected. From their vantage point, we were just two small kids locked in a moving embrace that carried us back and forth from one far corner of the rink to the other, first zigging, then zagging, then jumping, then spinning, all the while pumping our little legs as fast as they would go.

In one of our early competitions, Johnny had us skate against older children for the experience and practice. Knowing we'd be trounced and disappointed, he had Good Sportsmanship trophies made for each of us. When the judges tallied their points, all of us were shocked when Mickey and I won third place. That day we walked out with two giant trophies and noticeably swelled heads. We were a king and queen.

Things didn't always go so well, however. Prior to one competition, Mickey's mother was unable to finish his costume on time. Our coach rushed us toward the rink as she sewed another row of sequins onto his sleeve and then pinned his cuff to hold it together.

"Mom!" he cried out.

"Hurry up, you're late," she said.

"But—"

"Don't talk. Just get out on the floor."

He winced throughout the routine, skated to the "Imperial Waltz." I could tell something was wrong, drastically wrong. But I didn't know what until we finished our routine. Stepping off the rink, Mickey raced over to his mother and held up his arm. Blood soaked his cuff. A look of horror crossed her face as she saw what she had done. In her rush she'd pinned the cuff to his wrist!

The night before each meet, my father dismantled my skates atop a blanket of newspaper on the kitchen table. He cleaned the wheels with a Q-tip to remove dust and grease, oiled the eight ball bearings in each, and then put the pieces back together. He wanted me to have every chance to win. And if I lost, he expected me to hold my head high.

At that age, I didn't understand losing the way my father did. As I saw it, either Mickey and I got the trophy or somebody else did. After losing one meet, I dashed into the rest room in tears. I wanted the trophy but couldn't have it.

The moment I came out, my father grabbed me firmly by the arm and sat me down hard on a nearby bench. "If you can't lose like a champion, you'll never skate again," he said. "Take off your skates now, because you'll never go on the floor again."

I sniffled and wiped my eyes as he continued. "I am very, very proud of you, Susie. But I won't tolerate a bad loser. The team that beat you worked much harder, and it paid off for them. So don't cry because you lost or because they were better. You aren't skating to beat them. You skate to beat yourself—to do better than you did before. If you win, pat yourself on the back. If you lose, keep your head high, and then go out and work harder."

Though Mickey and I skated well together, we drove each other crazy a good deal of time. Before one state championship meet, a dance was held for all partici-pants and their parents. Neither Mickey nor I could dance, so our parents practiced box steps with us all af-ternoon.

I knew it was a strain for Mickey to be nice too long. Sure enough, his politeness disintegrated midway through the evening dance when he began squeezing my hand like a sponge. I stomped his foot in return, and he pinched me hard. I yelled and slugged him square in the belly. That got his attention, but not for long. The rest of the night, we tried to kill each other right there amidst the sedate, two-stepping crowd.

Like a mismatched couple, we had our irreconcilable differences. When I wanted to skate fast, he went slow. If I wanted to practice, he refused. If I was in a serious mood, he goofed off. We broke up a dozen times, vow-ing never to skate together again. But we always made up before the next meet, and Mickey would bring me a stuffed animal as a peace offering and for good luck.

Mickey and I did well in pairs competition, but I actu-ally did better on my own. There was a direct trade off between the hours I spent practicing and how well I did. If I lost, I could only blame myself.

As a freestyle skater, I won enough ribbons at local and area events to qualify for the state meet. The first year I tried, I came in second. The next year I skated even better, performing at full-throttle speed. As the first child to complete a series of five critical jumps in consecutive order, I knew I had the inside track.

Working up to rocket speed, I began with a waltz jump, making a half turn in the air and landing backward on the opposite skate. Upon touchdown, I kicked airborne into a full turn loop, followed by a reverse Mapes, which sent me spinning the opposite direction. Then came a full-turn Euler, which led straight to the final backward rotation Salchow. I felt as light as an angel, and I didn't make any mistakes. But the other competitors didn't seem to make mistakes either.

Mom was with me in the ladies' locker room as I awaited the judges' decision and changed for the trip home. It was about midnight and the winners had still not been announced. Suddenly the locker room door burst open and my father, beaming a smile, sprinted to my side. He grabbed me in his arms and held me tight.

"We won!" his lips shouted, tears streaming down his face. And then he hugged Mom and me together, crying and repeating over and over, "We won! We won! We won!" as other women looked on and smiled. At seven years old, I was the Ohio state champion!

After winning the state championship, my parents carted me around to exposition meets in nearby states in preparation for the regionals. In Milwaukee, Wisconsin, I met a group of high school skaters from Peoria, Illinois. We skated together for a month and got to know each other well. As the youngest, I was the group's mascot.

Of all the skaters, I liked Judy Clark the best. I'd often told Mom I wanted a sister, someone I could talk with rather than fight with as I did with my brothers. Mom just smiled and said I had to be content with the siblings God had given me.

During that special time leading up to the regional competition, Judy became the big sister I'd always wanted. A muscular five-foot-six, with short, curly hair, Judy had dark, soft eyes that mirrored her warmth and gentleness. We quickly developed a close bond, and it seemed as if we'd known each other our entire lives. She calmed me with notes before each meet and hugged me afterward whether I won or lost.

"You're the best," she told me again and again as the championship in Pontiac, Michigan, approached.

When the day of the regionals finally arrived, however, I was a nervous wreck. At stake was a trip to California for the nationals. When my turn came, my hands were cold and sweaty. It wasn't butterflies I had in my stomach; it was bats.

From the far end of the rink, I watched Johnny's hand drop. Once I was on the roll, my nerves quit jumping. I felt good. People were smiling. Everything would be fine. We'd rehearsed hundreds times, and I could have performed blindfolded.

I skated forward, easing into a camel and stretching my right leg back until it was level with my head. *Hold it, one, two, then a three-turn snap into reverse, picking up speed. Slide into a sweeping heel-to-heel mohawk turn. Cross, blast forward, and—careful now!—hit the jumps: the waltz, loop, Mapes, Euler, Salchow. Yahoo! See the happy people, everybody clapping and going crazy!*

Circle back, shift into reverse, rise up on the right leg, and then hit a sit spin. Head up, forward, speed, then another waltz, a Salchow, an outside one-foot spin, another

mohawk, and then lead into a graceful two-foot spin.
Move toward the side of the rink, smile at the happy,
happy crowd, and then . . . and then . . . And then what?
Mind blank. Blanker than blank. Snow white blank.

In panic, I glanced back at Johnny. He waved for me
to continue skating. Then my eyes darted to my parents, standing in the middle along the half wall. Judy
was beside them, motioning me to keep going.

What now? Dear God, what now? Whatever you do,
don't skate off the rink. No tears. No choice but go back
to the beginning. Start over again.

I could see people still applauding, unaware I was in
big trouble. Nothing like this had ever happened to me
before. I'd never forgotten my routine. I'd been ninety
seconds from winning the trip to California, but now. . .

I faked a bright smile and started over—repeating my
spectacular jumps for the second flawless time. But at
the midpoint, I again went blank. So I began the routine yet another time, remembering how my father had
always said never to quit in the middle. Only the music
quit—music I couldn't hear.

When I glanced into the stands again, the cheering
had stopped. Everybody was looking back and forth at
each other. Some were laughing. I kept skating—until I
suddenly noticed Johnny walking toward me in the
rink, motioning me off the floor.

"It's over, Susie," his lips said. "The music ended."
Draping his arm around me, he led me off the floor
with tears in his eyes as hundreds of people looked on.

I was surprised to see Mom and Dad were also crying. Mom ran toward me and threw her arms around
my neck.

"I'm sorry," I said.

She pulled back and wiped her eyes. "There's nothing to be sorry about, Susie. I don't know why certain things happen, but God will show us in time."

After losing the regional title, I was especially disheartened because Judy and the other exposition skaters all won their divisions. I was the only one who would not make the trip to Oakland in August. No suitcase, no gypsy hours on the road, no license plate games, no basking in the light of Judy's friendship, no trophy.

When Judy and the others left for California, I eagerly awaited a letter from her telling me she'd won and describing the trophy. She said she'd write, but her letter never came.

The day after nationals, as I worked out at the local rink, I saw Mom out of the corner of my eye. She was standing with her arms around Mickey. I wondered what was wrong but really didn't care. My mind was thousands of miles away with Judy.

A few minutes later, Mom waved me to the sidelines. As I approached, I noticed her eyes were red and wet.

"Take off your skates. We're going home," she said.

"Why?"

"Please, just take them off."

As I sat on a bench and unlaced my skates, I asked what was wrong.

"There's been an accident."

"What? Who?" I felt my heart lurch in my throat.

"It's Judy."

"Judy!"

"Johnny just got the phone call."

"She'll be OK, won't she?"

Mom shook her head.

"She's my best friend. Say she'll be OK! Please say yes, Mom! Please!"

"She's gone, Susie."

"Gone where?"

In the next instant, I saw the answer in her eyes as she glanced down.

"Susie, Judy is dead."

"How could—" But I couldn't finish the sentence or thought, and didn't say anything all the way home. I just sat in my seat, numb and alone, as large, heavy tears coursed down my cheeks.

When we finally got home, Mom explained that Judy's car had been sideswiped on a bridge by a big truck. After the collision, the car barrelled through the guardrail and plunged three stories into the water. Judy apparently died instantly, along with another skater. Two others had been seriously injured.

The following day as I cried in my room, Mom came and sat beside me. She turned my head so I could see her lips. "Susie, do you remember what I said in Pontiac? That we can't know why certain things happen, but there's a reason for everything?"

I nodded.

"If you hadn't forgotten your routine, you probably would have been in that car."

I nodded again.

"You are alive only by the grace of God. I don't understand it all and probably never will. But, Susie, God must have big plans for your life."

Shortly after Judy's funeral, her mother sent me a newspaper picture of Judy with her national championship trophy. She was standing beside the other three winners, proud and smiling—unaware she'd be dead within twenty-four hours of the flash of the camera.

Years later I had the photo framed. It sits in my office today, near Miss Vetterle's, as a memento of a special friendship and as a constant reminder of the brevity of life and things I don't understand.

At any moment, we are all one step from eternity. Why some people's paths are shorter than others' is, for now, only for God to know. It's on my list of questions to ask him someday.

If there are skates in heaven, I hope Judy is there—with her Douglas Snyders oiled and laced, ready for a few laps with the one who loved her like a sister.

7

THE DUMMY CLASS

n early elementary school, I was tested to see how I compared academically with other children across the country. The annual test, known as the Iowa Record Exam, supposedly measured basic skills in language and math; I viewed it merely as an art project and a welcomed break in the normal classroom routine.

As I worked my way down through the multiple choice questions, I marked the tiny little answer boxes that helped create the most interesting patterns. I didn't bother with whether my answer was right or wrong, because all the answers looked right. When it came to the correct spelling of Mississippi or the sum of three-digit numbers, I really didn't know. I just wanted to make pretty patterns.

When I was finished, my answer sheet was a beautiful collection of little penciled rectangles cutting diagonally to the right, then to the left, then straight down. I was always so proud when I finished and equally distraught when I was scored in the lowest percentile of students.

When I took the results home to my parents, they both cried. No matter how many times I took the test in subsequent years, I never improved. My self-esteem was shattered. I began to think everybody was right: I was a certified dummy. The test results proved it.

If I was as stupid as the test indicated, I couldn't understand why Mom forced me to waste endless hours doing homework when I could have been playing.

"Am I stupid?" I asked her one day.

"Of course not," she said.

"I see you cry when I bring home the tests."

"I cry because I see how hard you try. I cry because the tests don't measure what really matters. They don't measure your determination or kindness. They don't measure how big your heart is. They don't measure how wide your love stretches. They measure none of these things, so they measure nothing at all."

"So I'm not stupid?"

"Dear heart, the *tests* are stupid."

Nevertheless, in the third grade I was enrolled in a special class, widely known as the Dummy Class. My classmates consisted of a ragtag bunch of slow learners and those with various handicaps and deformities. One boy had cerebral palsy and an oversized head; another had a dragging foot and a twisted, paralyzed arm tucked by his side. One girl wore Good Will dresses that never fit; another spent large blocks of time at her desk praying aloud with her eyes closed and hands folded. There was also an assortment of bullies who had flunked a grade or two and worked out their frustrations by rearranging the faces of younger children.

From that point on, I was marked as being stupid to everybody but Mom. "Hey, dummy!" I was taunted before class, on breaks, during recess, and after school.

"The dummy can't even talk right!" kids from regular classrooms said, making faces and mimicking the way I sounded. "Thuthie, Thuthie, panth on fire, hanging by a telephone wire!"

I tried the comeback my brothers taught me about how sticks and stones could break my bones, but words could never hurt me. It was a lie, of course. The words hurt like daggers.

My teachers attempted to assuage some of the pain by appointing me blackboard monitor or letting me grade papers during recess. One year I was even asked to demonstrate my skating ability in the gym for all the students in my class. Those small encouragements nourished me for weeks. But my schoolyard detractors, led by Jimmy and Raymond, were hardly impressed.

When I saw the band of boys coming my way, I deliberately turned around or sought safety in another group of kids. I thought I'd find refuge in the huddle, but it merely increased the number of people who witnessed my embarrassment. Other times I ran back to the classroom, only to have the recess teacher stop me and make me stay on the playground. When I couldn't avoid them, I was usually forced to fight. Once the fists were flying, I wanted to knock their heads off.

The closest I came to doing that was when I clobbered Jimmy in the face with my balled-up fist. As usual, I got spanked by the principal. But I felt exonerated the following day when Jimmy showed up with a shiner as big as a saucepan. And I felt no greater thrill than to see him teased for having gotten a black eye from a girl. That was revenge at its best.

Soon thereafter, Jimmy was waiting for me after school at the bus stop. "Hey, dodo bird," he said, shoving me when I came within reach.

I pushed him away and he laughed.

"Thheee . . . Thhpod . . . rruunnn," he said, calling up horrid memories from preceding years. Then he pulled one of my pigtails.

I whipped around to clobber him, but he wasn't there. Then he pulled my other pigtail. I reeled back suddenly and, without too much thought, smashed my notebook into his face. It caught him square on the nose. A look of profound pain crossed his face, and his hand shot to his nose. When he pulled it away, it was dripping with blood. Tears flowed down his face as he turned tail and ran into the arms of the teacher on duty. She held him, stroked his head, and said some secret things in his ear. When she looked up at me, there was disgust in her eyes.

A dizzy confusion of emotion swept over me. I saw the compassion Jimmy got, the warm words, the pats. Everybody ran to him and tried to comfort him. They saw his pain, but not mine. He was taken to the nurse, while I was dragged to the office.

After my mother was phoned, the school secretary led me into the principal's office. As I stood before his desk, he listed the charges against me. I had a behavior problem, his lips said. I couldn't get along with other kids, his lips said. It was my fault, his lips said. My grades were dropping, his lips said. Perhaps I should consider a transfer to a deaf school, his lips said.

"I won't let kids make fun of me!" I cried. "Jimmy started it. He shoved me and pulled my hair and laughed at me. I didn't just go out there and hit him!"

"But you can't keep fighting with boys. You're a girl. Girls don't do these things!" And then he reached for the paddle, motioned me to the side of his desk, and gave me a solid, stinging swat.

When Mom arrived, she talked alone with the principal. As soon as we were in the car she turned to face me. "Something has got to change, Susie," she said.

"I won't let them laugh at me!"

"You don't understand. You can't keep fighting."

"They won't make fun of me! I won't let them!"

She shook her head and turned away as tears clouded her eyes. I glared out the window as anger boiled and steamed within my calloused heart. I wanted to scream, to lash out, to get even. Most of all, I wanted to turn back the clock to the years before I started school when nobody seemed to think I was different, back when I had friends and was still understood.

That night after dinner, my parents drew me aside. They had a serious look on their faces, and I thought I was in trouble. "Susie, we have something to ask you," my father began. "But before we do, we want you to know the choice is yours. If it's something you want, you can do it. If not, that's fine too."

I just looked at him, not understanding what he was getting at. I glanced at Mom's lips.

"Your principal has suggested that we put you in a deaf school," she said. "You'd be just like all the other kids. No more laughing and fighting. You'd have a chance to learn."

"A deaf school?" I asked. "Where nobody can hear?"

They both nodded.

"Where?"

"New Orleans."

"We'd move?"

"No, it's a boarding school. You'd live there. That's the choice you have to make."

I shook my head. The choice was easy. I couldn't leave my parents. Home was where my heart was.

"Your doctors think it would be good for you," Mom said. "There are fine clinics near the school, and—"

"No, I'm not going," I said.

They both looked at each other and nodded. Nothing more was said, and the subject never again came up.

About that time, I was fitted for hearing aids that were hidden in the ear pieces of my glasses. When I cranked them up full blast, I occasionally heard a faint, faraway *buzz*. But my everyday world remained absolutely silent. I was still deaf to people talking, phones ringing or doors slamming. I couldn't have heard a jet take off if I was standing beside it.

Whenever doctors and audiologists asked me what the buzz sounded like, I didn't know what to say. It was the only sound I knew, so there was nothing with which to compare it. They might just as well have asked a blind person to describe the color black. You can't say it's dark if you don't know what *light* is, or that it's like the night if you've never seen the *day*.

Their question reminded me of the morning Mom entered my room, pulled the shade, opened the window, and sat beside me as I rubbed my eyes awake. Her radiant face was often singing in the morning, but that particular day she just stared out the window with a faraway look in her eyes.

"What is it, Mom?"

"Nothing, Sweetheart."

"Tell me. You're thinking something."

"Oh, little Susie," she said, stroking my leg. "I was just wishing you could hear the birds. They're singing now, and they sound so beautiful."

"Tell me what they sound like."

"Their beaks go up and down," she said, moving her thumb and forefinger together in tight, little pinching motions. "And the sound they make is like . . . well, like music, like a clarinet and flute duet, like—"

"What does a clarinet sound like? And a flute? What does it sound like?"

"Oh, sort of like a rushing mountain stream."

"Tell me what a stream sounds like, Mom."

"Like . . . like . . . ," she began, but her words trailed off as her lips stopped moving. At that moment she smiled at me with a sad smile. "Like a bird, dear heart."

Then I knew her problem. She couldn't describe a sound without comparing it to another sound, and I was deaf to them all. The same thing happened one day when I was sitting in the bathtub, feeling the water gush from the faucet at my feet. I held my hand beneath the torrent, and it was batted away.

"Boy, it's so strong!" I said to Mom. When I asked her what it sounded like, she thought for a moment, and then said, "Like a roar." She opened her mouth wide and drew her hands up like claws. "Like a lion," she added.

I, of course, knew neither the sound of a roar or of a lion. The only sounds I understood were those I could feel. In the summer when we had huge storms, I sat by the window and watched the lightning for hours. I never got scared. Once I even slept like a baby through a tornado because I never heard the winds. But during one storm when the streets were turned into rivers and great bolts of lightning ripped across the sky every minute, the house began to shake. I glanced at Mom with panic in my eyes.

"That's thunder," she said.

From that point on, I associated thunder with the shaking of a house. Thunder I could feel. But I couldn't feel the song of a bird, the music of a flute, the sound of a mountain stream, or the roar of a lion.

Though I could hear nothing meaningful with the aids, I kept them turned to full volume just in case. However, my parents continually motioned me to turn them down because they said they emitted a high-pitched "whistle"—particularly at the dinner table when I was eating and moved my jaw a certain way.

I soon learned I could cause the sound simply by yawning or moving my mouth at just the right angle, which I occasionally did when I was bored in class. It was quite humorous to watch the teacher suddenly stop and raise her head.

"What's that sound?" she'd say. The other students would look around, but with an imperceptible twitch of my jaw I'd shut off the whistle, and everybody would shrug and resume their work. I kept this up for several days until I finally started to laugh.

The teacher eyed me suspiciously. "Susan, is that you making the sound?" she asked.

"What sound?" I replied innocently. "I can't hear a thing!"

We generally had the first good snow before Thanksgiving, when our home was filled with the smell of turkey, special breads, and pumpkin, apple and cherry pies. The holiday smells and spirit carried through Christmas, when we devoted an entire day to hanging tinsel, ornaments, lights, and popcorn strings on the tree. Underneath it we created a small town and set up a working Lionel train.

Many blizzards ripped through Boardman, gathering speed and moisture from the nearby Great Lakes and turning our crab-apple-tree war zone of summer and autumn into an icy battlefield. My brothers and I spent hours building snow forts and stockpiling a cache of wall-to-wall snowballs, which were thrown with the force of Wayne Gretzky slap shots. As the frequent target, I often ran for cover inside, where I'd warm up by the furnace, get some encouragement from Mom, and then head straight back to the front lines.

Mill Creek Park was one of my favorite places. My whole family often dragged our sleds there on still winter nights and posted candles on the slopes to mark our course. It was the best of times: sledding headfirst atop my dad at suicide speeds, roping toboggans to the car and being towed through the park, making snow angels beneath a backdrop of giant, snow-laden pines, and then finally, wearily trudging home, stripping off wet clothes, and drinking hot cocoa around the fireplace. It was the best of times, indeed.

For me as a child in the 1950s, Youngstown was my New York. My favorite outing was going downtown to Strauss and McKelvey's, a department store crowded with everything I could ever need and possibly want. Walking through the aisles with my eyes missing nothing, I filled my lungs with the smells of new shiny bikes, bright red wagons, white almond chocolate, and best of all, hot buttered popcorn.

The sights and smells were so different from those outside, where steel mill blast furnaces belched flames and acrid smoke from endless rows of chimneys. People scurried amidst the sooty infernos, working at the same sweaty, feverish pace as did, in my imagination, devils in hell.

When we strolled through the department store at Christmas, Mom would often cock her head a certain way and slow her walk. Sometimes she'd stop in the middle of an aisle and her eyes would begin to glisten. Then she'd give me that look of hers, stoop down, draw me close with a big hug, and not let me go. At such times, I knew there was music playing in the store.

"What are they playing?" I'd ask, and she'd tell me either "The First Noel," "Oh Come, All Ye Faithful," "Silent Night," or some other such song. Without her having to tell me, I knew she felt pain deep inside because I would never hear the music, the church choir carolers who roamed the mall, the Salvation Army lady with her bucket and bell, or the trumpet ensemble posted outside.

"Its OK, Mom," I'd say, giving her hand a squeeze and pulling her toward the toy store.

On Christmas Eve, our family dressed up and headed to church. Its steeple was tall and white; its pews, hard as boulders. I got goose bumps when the sanctuary lights were dimmed, candles lit, and we sang my personal anthem, "Silent Night." With hundreds of tiny flames dancing around me and the church filled with the scent of pine and cologne and dark, rich wood, I sang at the top of my lungs. I heard nothing, but felt an abiding peace deep in my soul as all my hurts and frustrations from Dummy Class evaporated into the rafters. Jimmy and Raymond seemed like bygone memories. All was calm; all was bright.

When we got home, I crawled into bed—awakening on Christmas dawn to mountains of brightly wrapped boxes beneath the tree. As a child, the magnificence of that huge mound of presents seemed too good to be true, and I never quite understood how it all worked. It was Jesus' birthday, but I got all the gifts. Was that a great religion, or what!

8

LESSONS FOR LIFE

very week toward the end of winter, I checked the planter outside our living room window for signs of life. It was my seasonal thermometer. When the yellow daffodils burst through the snow on their long green stems, they heralded the hope that spring and the glories of Easter were soon to come, providing that Mr. Groundhog did not see his shadow.

Spring brought to Boardman the smell of cherry blossoms, green grass, and little growing things. It was a time when the wind stopped blowing, paint quit peeling, and snow ceased falling. The trees sprouted tiny green banners of new life, dandelions raised their heads, and we began grooming the garden—turning, hoeing, and planting the thick, black soil. Every family member had a job in the garden. Mine was to sprinkle seeds in the trenches plowed by my father.

The advent of spring also brought warmer weather, fresh sunshine, and kites. Dad helped me make huge, peacock-colored kites, with long flappy tails torn from painting rags, that soared till they touched the clouds. Dad never took shortcuts. Whatever he did, he did perfectly. His kites were no exception; they sailed the skies like clipper ships.

Every spring Dad either washed or painted the inside of the house, and every other summer until his eightieth birthday, he painted the outside. To him, cleanliness *was* next to godliness. When he finally called another painter to do the outside, he stuck closer to him than the man's shadow.

"There. Over there," he'd say, pointing to a spot under the eaves that didn't get full coverage, or where a mite had landed in the paint, or where the brush stroke was not quite even. The other man was a true saint by the way he allowed Dad to boss and tail him, all the while talking about his own bygone customers who demanded—and *got*—perfection.

As the weather warmed, our family sometimes traveled to Coldwater, Michigan, to visit Mom's parents. Grandpa Meyers was a dairy farmer who traveled from farm to farm looking for work. There never was much money, but they had a small cottage on Lake Morrison, so they seemed rich.

One lazy afternoon in Coldwater, I tagged along when my brother Paul and his buddy, Nicky Schilinger, headed for the dock to fish. My cousin Sharon, who'd contracted polio at a young age and wore a brace on one leg, also joined us.

Fishing off the end of the dock with a gob of worms, Paul and Nicky both had a couple of catfish hooked within the hour. I didn't get so much as a nibble, however, and pulled the worm out of the water every five minutes to check whether it was still alive.

"You ain't gonna catch nothin' that way. Fish don't jump that high," Nicky said, his lips moving faster than I could understand.

"What did he say?" I asked, turning to my brother.

"Said put your hook back in the water."

"The worm's dead."

"Of course it's dead, stupid. But that don't make any difference to a dumb fish."

"Stupid! You called her stupid!" Sharon said, bracing her hand on her hip. "I'm telling when we get home."

"OK, she's not stupid."

"I think fish like live worms better than dead worms," I commented, dropping my line over the edge of the dock and watching the worm disappear into the murky water two feet below.

"You ain't gonna catch nothin' that way neither. Them's just beer cans down there," Nicky said, his lips racing. "The fish, they're out there aways," he added, pointing farther out in the lake.

I looked to my brother for understanding.

"Said you need to cast," he repeated. "Here, watch me." He flipped his rod back over his shoulder, and with a snap of his wrist he sent his worm and bobber flying. They landed with a splash about thirty feet away, sending doughnut ripples back to the dock. "Man, I ought to go professional," he beamed, glancing back to see if I was watching his lips. "Lots of people would pay for me to teach them how to cast like that and tell them the best bait and show them where the secret spots are and where the big mothers hang out."

I looked at him and nodded. He smiled big at me and then drew me over to learn from the master. "You saw how I did it, Susie. Now you try it. Do it just like me. It's all in the wrist."

I again pulled the line up, examined the soggy worm's vital signs, and then threw the baited hook behind me. I spread my feet, fingered the reel, and stretched my pole way back over my shoulder. Grabbing the base with two hands, I gave the rod a couple of test jerks. And then, just as I braced for a mighty cast and my nerves were all twitchy, something very big and powerful slammed into me, knocking me off my feet.

It felt like I'd been hit by a truck, and the force of the blow sent me sliding. My fingers scratched for a hold. They pawed at the dock. I didn't want to fall in the water. What hit me was now holding me and was all over my back. I struggled to free myself, screaming and kicking and crying all at the same time. I felt hot blasts of breath on my neck.

"Get off me!" I yelled, hoping others could hear. I glanced over my shoulder suddenly. Out of the side of my eyes, I saw it was Nicky. I didn't understand what was happening, and my back was sore where he hit me.

Rising to my knees, I reached for my pole. But he again slammed me to the dock, knocking the pole from my hands. My heart beat tattoos in my throat. I was too stunned to speak. He pinned my arms till I thought they would break. Paul snatched my rod from the deck beside me. His face looked angry. I sputtered for him to get his smelly gorilla friend off me, but he ignored my voice.

Suddenly I felt Nicky release his clamp grip. I jumped to my feet, ready to knock his head off with my pole.

"What are you doing?" I screamed.

He motioned behind himself.

I couldn't understand what he was indicating, so I shouted the question again. This time he grabbed me by the arm and dragged me a few steps closer to where the others were hunched and pointed again.

"Forget them, why did you knock me down? Tell me! What's going on?"

His lips called me a stupid idiot, and his finger kept jabbing the air in Sharon's direction. I glanced over. That's when I finally saw that Sharon was on the ground with a look of terror on her face. Something was obviously wrong. Something was in her eye.

It all flashed into my brain at once. What was in her eye was my big mush of lifeless worm; poking through her right eyelid, my barbed hook!

I buried my face in my hands so I wouldn't see her eye and what they were saying about me. But I knew what they were saying: deaf and dumb, deaf and dumb. And I was too. Nicky knew I was so deaf and dumb that I couldn't hear anybody's screams, so he mowed me down. What choice did he have? Otherwise, I would have ripped her eyelid right off.

The summer I turned nine, I enrolled in vacation Bible school at Evangel Baptist Church in Youngstown. I suppose my parents figured it was something the hearing kids did, and so they wanted me to go too. At one of the weekday musical programs, I was sitting in the back of the sanctuary with the older students. For an hour I sat there, getting nothing out of the program and breaking the monotony by pulling the hair of and elbowing the boys around me.

Suddenly, I felt the organ kick into the great hymn, "How Great Thou Art." That was our cue to depart, and I rose to leave with the others.

Halfway out, something stopped me. I felt the vibrations rising up through my feet, coursing through my bones and rolling about inside my head. My heart swelled, and tears flooded my eyes. I'd played the song at home and knew the vibrations and words by heart:

> *O Lord my God, when I in awesome wonder*
> *Consider all the worlds Thy hands have*
> *   made,*
> *I see the stars, I hear the rolling thunder,*
> *Thy pow'r thro'out the universe displayed.*
> *Then sings my soul, my Savior God, to Thee;*
> *How great Thou art, how great Thou art!*

Turning around, I walked slowly to the front of the church, drawn by the backlighted wooden cross. I disregarded everybody and everything else around me, shrugging off a hand on my shoulder. I had eyes only for the cross, which shimmered in its halo of warm light. Everything else was a blur. I felt my heart pounding in my chest. It felt ready to burst with joy and thankfulness and love—emotion that hit me as suddenly and unexpectedly as when Nicky had tackled me on the dock.

At the front of the church, I stopped at the altar. My eyes streamed tears down my cheeks as the hymn continued to beat up through my feet and deep, deep into my bones. My whole body was singing, though my lips were still.

As I surveyed the cross, I thought of my Jesus picture hanging on my wall at home, and how it had comforted and calmed me. I thought of the peace I felt when singing "Silent Night." I thought of the morning, years earlier, when I'd run into the backyard and fallen to my knees, praying that Jesus would one day bring my brother home. I thought of the power and glory I saw around me every day—a power that raised the daffodils in our yard every spring as surely as the sun every morning.

The cross and the one it once held seemed more real than ever before. In that moment they became personal and alive. The power that made all the worlds, the stars, and the rolling thunder was mine. Finally I spoke.

"Someday I'm going to build you a church," I said, mouthing silent, prayerful words. "Someday I'm going to build you a church."

The words came straight from my heart and out of my mouth without me knowing exactly what I was praying about or what the words meant. I didn't think I'd build a church in the literal sense, but I wanted to do something with my life that mattered in the face of eternity. Maybe I would become a missionary. Or a nun. Perhaps the church I'd build would be more figurative—a group of people like myself. I didn't really know. I just knew that somehow God had a plan for my life that exceeded my understanding at that young age—a plan that would not be hindered by my deafness.

I've never lost the memory of that precious moment, and I'm grateful that others like it have been repeated in my life. Now when I sit in church, tears frequently stream down my face when I feel the vibrations of a particular hymn rise up through the floor and I watch those around me singing. For those few minutes, the stresses of life are erased from their everyday faces. Lines of worry and frustration disappear. Hope and promise are restored. The transformation is as supernatural as the arrival of spring, and I see in their eyes a glimmer of heaven.

As I passed through that stage called childhood, I never had time to complain of boredom, for my childhood disappeared in a rush of lessons and tutors and such things as vacation Bible school and Girl Scouts. I eventually realized that whatever I wanted to do—and some things that I didn't—my parents would provide the opportunity.

I liked to swim, so Mom enrolled me in lessons at the community pool. But with twenty-five people in the class and the teacher talking from the pool deck, it was impossible for me to read lips and understand what was going on. So my father took some extra jobs, and Mom arranged for a private teacher. With that one-on-one instruction, I no longer felt like a fish out of water.

When Paul entered the army, he left his trumpet behind, and Mom began giving me daily lessons at home after I had finished my piano lesson. The music lessons reflected Mom's interest, and she was determined that we both pay the price and take the time to see me become accomplished. She first taught me how to make vibrations in the mouthpiece, and then to play crude scales and simple songs. As with my piano lessons, I developed slowly but steadily. By junior high, I had bested twelve other young trumpeters and was playing first trumpet, third chair.

I also spent summers in school, learning to read and then improving my ability. Later, I progressed to speed reading and typing classes. I don't know whether my parents realized it at the time, but reading would eventually become my primary means of learning. Through books, my boundaries were moved back, and I realized that my potential and my world were unlimited. And with the development of special keyboard telephones and relay operators for the deaf, typing would enable me to communicate with anybody in the country.

If my parents knew or suspected any of that, I certainly didn't. I just experienced the frustration of not having much free time. When my neighborhood friends came over and asked if I could play, Mom had a standard answer that she adapted slightly depending on the time of year or my age: "No, Susie is practicing her music." "No, Susie is leaving to go skating." "No, Susie is heading for the pool." Pretty soon, they just stopped asking if Susie could play.

After my speech work with Miss Vetterle, my next major step in therapy was voice lessons, which I began at age ten. My teacher was Miss Amy Ackleson, an antique, gray-haired woman who preferred the lived-in look to makeup, and who accentuated everything she said with dramatic, sweeping hand movements.

In contrast to the iron-willed Miss Vetterle, Miss Ackleson was pure grandmother. She was neither stern nor critical, and I sensed it was all right with her if I just had fun and learned nothing. Consequently, I learned a lot.

We held court together on the old porch of her town-house, which she'd walled in and converted to a music room. The porch was dominated by a baby grand piano, as the living room was by an organ. Though a serious musician, she never forced me to share her passion, proceed faster than I was able, or be anything other than what I was: a girl who couldn't hear herself speak, let alone sing. At the same time, she did her best to instill in me a love for musical vibrations. And she was spunky enough that, along the way, she accomplished what she was paid for: to teach me how to play the piano well, vary the pitch of my monotonal voice, and even halfway carry a tune.

The voice lessons consisted of singing long stretches of scales, beginning with *ma, ma, ma, ma* . . . and continuing through *me, me, me, me* . . . to . . . *mo, mo, mo, mo*. In the summer when Miss Ackleson threw the windows open, passersby sometimes stopped and raised their heads, flashing bemused smiles before continuing on their way.

With my hand on the side of the piano to feel vibrations, I moved up the scales and down again, back and forth, trying my best to hit the right key while ignoring the outsiders. As we moved up the scale, Miss Ackleson's eyebrows climbed dramatically up her forehead until, at the peak, they seemed to merge with her hairline. When I hit a particularly bad note, they nearly jumped off her face. I can't imagine what we sounded like together, but I'm sure angels cringed and neighborhood dogs were set howling.

Two years after I began voice lessons, Miss Ackleson retired. My next stage of speech therapy was with Bertha Martin, a short, fat woman in her late forties whose dark brown hair was as kinky as a Brillo pad. She wore long dresses that looked like a Sears pup tent to cover her near-three-hundred-pound bulk. Despite her weight, she moved with great haste and was slowed only by the flight of stairs leading to her second-floor apartment.

Stacked floor to ceiling throughout her flat were piles of newspapers, magazines, and thick, dusty books that would normally be found either in the trash, in a dark corner of a garage, or in the attic. Rather than discard things she considered interesting, she piled them in corners, and then piled piles atop each other until the paper towers reached the ceiling.

The first time Mom dropped me off, a look of abject horror flashed in her eyes upon crossing the threshold. And though she expressed deep reservations about continuing the sessions, she acknowledged that Miss Martin's references checked out and seemed to outweigh the health risks involved.

Miss Martin was a woman, people said, who "really knew her stuff." A concert pianist and drama coach, albeit of bygone years, she had nevertheless played and worked in New York and had yellowed newspaper clippings to prove it. And that meant something in our little Boardman, Ohio.

My Wednesday afternoon lessons were conducted in her kitchen atop a rusty metal table, which was covered with breakfast leftovers, half-eaten pastries and cookie crumbs, legions of ants, several days of old mail, empty milk cartons, and several dated magazines—all of which she merely pushed off to the side so we could sit down.

Our sessions began with an hour of poetry reading, which was supposed to help with my articulation and enunciation. Rather than feeding me a diet of Mother Goose, she gorged me with meaty works by Rudyard Kipling and Robert Frost, and served up side dishes of such Shakespearean sonnets as:

> *When, in disgrace with fortune and*
> *   men's eyes,*
> *I alone beweep my outcast state*
> *And trouble deaf heaven with my*
> *   bootless cries*
> *And look upon myself and curse my fate,*
> *Wishing me like to one more rich in hope,*
> *Featur'd like him, like him with friends*
> *   possess'd,*
> *Desiring this man's art and that man's*
> *   scope,*
> *With what I most enjoy contented least;*
> *Yet in these thoughts myself almost*
> *   despising,*
> *Hap'ly I think on thee, and then my state,*
> *Like to the lark at break of day arising*
> *From sullen earth, sings hymns at*
> *   heaven's gate;*
> *For thy sweet love rememb'red such*
> *   wealth brings*
> *That then I scorn to change my state*
> *   with kings.*

I had no idea what most of it meant, and told her so. She encouraged me to think of the materials as nutritious brain food. If I ate what she set before me, the understanding would eventually come.

For weeks on end we studied and rehearsed such poetry. Again and again she would stop me midsentence, saying, "Once more, but with *feeling*." She was big on the dramatics of poetry, and when she recited the sonnet she put her whole body into it. My eyes were wide as I watched her breathe life into what had been, to me, mere words on paper. All three hundred pounds of her suddenly became animated—her face, arms, hands, and shoulders weaving and twisting and bobbing with exaggerated expression.

I would pick up the piece again, struggling to capture a fraction of her theatrics and feeling a surge of emotion at the end when I, looking to her for approval, would see a smile break over her face and her hands erupt in applause.

Wednesday poetry sessions were followed by an hour of piano in her living room, and under her tutelage I caught a glimpse of a whole new world. This world was expanded on periodic outings to fine restaurants and to the library, where I learned some of the finer things about life and the Dewey decimal system.

Every other month on a Saturday, Miss Martin piled two other students and myself into her car and drove us to the Youngstown Public Library. Once inside the doors, she would have us pause and inhale deeply the rich, warm smells of knowledge, which were better, she said, than the aroma of freshly baked bread. We then proceeded to a quiet table, where she told us to take a long, slow look around us. I turned my head, but all I saw were books.

"Don't you love it!" she said.

I shrugged.

"Books! Books! And more books! This library is stocked full with the food and fire for your mind. If you want to know how to train your dog or build a tree house; if you want information about chocolate factories or submarines; if you seek adventures to the Amazon jungles or the valleys of the moon . . . well, this is the place. It's all contained in books. And who you become five years from now will be determined, in part, by the books you read today."

She then pulled two long wooden drawers from the card catalog files, set them on the table in front of us, and explained how titles were indexed. And then, like a hen leading her chicks, she escorted us on treasure hunts through the maze of stacks to find a particular book. She gradually had us search out the titles ourselves, building up our confidence until the final day when she handed each of us a list of twenty different titles—from Hans Christian Andersen novels and Robert Burns poetry to Edgar Allan Poe collections and Shakespearean plays—which we were to seek out and retrieve. An hour later when we each returned, staggering with a stack of books we could barely see over, she beamed as if we were explorers who had discovered the secret of the universe.

On alternate Saturdays, Miss Martin treated us to lunch at the most exclusive restaurants in our small town, which meant getting dressed up in Sunday school finery. More than just a teacher's treat, the excursion was her attempt to teach us three students everyday etiquette: Which fork to eat a salad with. Where to put your elbows. How to be a polite conversationalist. What to do with the napkin after the meal. Miss Martin knew it all. Her knowledge was transferred and would one day enable me to feel comfortable with some of the wealthiest, most dignified people in the world.

I never forgot her lessons, and when I sometimes catch myself slouching during a meal or eating with my elbows on the table, I smile to myself with fond memories of a unique, spirited woman. If I'd been forced to choose between spending an afternoon with her or playing with the neighborhood kids, I'd have chosen her any day.

9

FAULT LINES

ver the next few years, my world changed more than I ever thought possible. The stability I had come to expect at home first began to tremble and then abruptly became fluid, just as ground seems to liquify in a major earthquake. When the once-solid foundation cracked open, my life tottered and reality came to rest at a crazy angle.

The first rumbling occurred about the time I entered Boardman Junior High School. Newly built, the front of the school had a fresh brick face, the dark beige woodwork and cream-colored walls were immaculately painted, and the desks had yet to be scratched or carved with initials. Everything smelled like a new car.

I enjoyed the hustle and bustle of changing classrooms and having my own locker, which was neatly arranged with my storehouse of books, Peachy files, notepads, a dozen needle-sharp, yellow Ticonderoga pencils, and a handful of Pink Pearl erasers. It was my private space, protected by a weighty, silver-and-black Master padlock, which only I could open with my secret combination.

However, my sense of privacy abruptly changed on a visit to my parents' friends in a nearby town. I thought of them like family and called them aunt and uncle. We always kissed them hello and good-bye. But when I kissed Uncle Keith that particular time, he forced his tongue into my mouth. I didn't understand what he was doing or why, but I was old enough to know it felt awful and nearly got sick to my stomach on the spot. That stolen kiss went unnoticed by my parents and, unfortunately, unreported by me as well.

That same visit, I was in their living room with my parents and said I was thirsty. Mom told me Uncle Keith was in the kitchen and would get me a drink. When I walked up to him, he turned around and gave me a big hug. There was nothing abnormal about that, until I realized he wouldn't let me go. He rubbed his body hard against me and put his hands on my chest. When I pushed him away, he gave me a drink of water as if nothing had happened, and I pretended the same when I returned to the living room.

The abuse continued for years, almost until he died. I did my best to keep my distance, but he seemed to know where I was at all times. When he trapped me in a room by myself, I pleaded with him not to touch me. "Please don't," I cried. Sometimes he was drunk and I could push him away. Other times I felt powerless.

When they visited our home, he and his wife slept in my room, and I stayed in the basement. There was a bathroom downstairs, and it wasn't unusual for people to use the extra shower. On one visit, Uncle Keith came down early in the morning when I was sound asleep. I didn't know he was there until I felt a hand nudge me awake. When I turned over and opened my eyes, he was standing naked before me.

I opened my mouth to scream, but the sound died in my throat. I quickly yanked the covers over my head and held on for dear life. Mom had never told me about this kind of thing. I felt trapped, unprepared for the moment. I couldn't flee. All I could do was not let go of the covers.

I clung to them, shaking, for an hour or more. My breaths came in spurts. Was he still beside me or had he gone back upstairs? I didn't know because I couldn't hear. When I finally dared to peek out, I was terrified. Though he was gone, I couldn't stop shaking. The worst part was feeling totally helpless. I was not safe even in my own house, and I had no idea where the earth would open next.

Maybe my terror would have stopped if I had merely told somebody. But I felt scared and ashamed. If I said something, I was afraid it would affect my parents. When they all got together, they laughed five years off their lives. I thought my parents would have no friends without them. I didn't want that because I knew what having no friends felt like, and it felt awful. So I said nothing, and in so doing I proved how dumb I truly was. Deaf and very dumb, indeed.

Mom was having troubles of her own during this period that would have a lasting and profound impact on my life. All along I'd been totally dependent on her. She was rock solid, or so I thought. As I became so painfully aware, certainties vanish when the earth cracks open.

At first I thought she was mad about something—maybe something that was my fault. She spent increasingly more time in her bedroom, refusing to come out for days at a time. Once she locked herself in for almost two weeks, and her mother had to take care of me.

I later sensed that her periods of isolation may have had nothing to do with me. I began to think they were triggered by problems on my dad's side of the family, but I couldn't be sure because I missed so much of what was discussed or experienced at home. Why was somebody happy? Why were they mad? I didn't know. What were their joys and pains? Why did they hurt? What did they feel? With my eyes, I heard only parts of their conversations some of the time, so I felt like an outsider even in my own home.

I spent endless hours trying to sort out the puzzle and figure out why things happened and people responded like they did. I ask questions even now, but nobody wants to participate in verbal archaeology. What they've kept from me all these years remains buried.

At the time, I didn't realize Mom's bedroom days were a signal—premonitory vibrations of the horror up ahead. They were a warning just before the ground lifted up.

The cataclysm hit when Grandma Thomas died. I was in the ninth grade. Our family got dressed up to go to the funeral home. The sadness of the moment was surpassed by my surprise of seeing my brother Billy there with his young family. I hadn't seen him since I was five, when Mom announced he didn't love us anymore and had run away from home.

He walked right up to me and said, "Hi, Susie," as if he'd just been gone for the weekend. My heart melted. My initial response was to run into his arms, hold him, and not let go. But I had been drilled by Mom that if anybody asked how many brothers I had, I was to say two. I could never say I had three. So in a confusion of emotion, I mumbled a quick hello in return and then just stood there shuffling my feet and smiling awkwardly.

When I got home, Dad reported that Billy and his wife were coming over. That was all it took. Mom promptly went to bed, crying. I instinctively knew it would be a long time before I'd see Billy again.

A few days later, Mom came out of her room in her nightgown. I ran up to her and could see that she was still crying. Her face was puffy and her hair was a mess. I threw my arms around her, but she just kept walking. I followed her down the steps into the basement laundry room where she pulled an old dusty rope out of the corner. I watched as she stood on a chair and tied one end around a rafter.

"Mom!" I screamed. "What are you doing? Mom, no!"

"Nobody loves me," she cried.

I ran and grabbed her by the legs. "Mom, I love you! I love you, Mom! Daddy does too. Everybody loves you!"

"Nobody, nobody, nobody!" her lips screamed as she grabbed a knot of her hair in her fist and pulled until I thought it would come out. Her tears fell down upon my face, mingling with my own as I hung on to her.

"I need you, Mom. Please, stop talking crazy!"

"This is the best thing I can do. Everybody would be happy."

Not knowing what else to do, I just squeezed my eyes shut and held onto her legs and screamed at the top of my lungs for as long as I could, screaming and screaming and hoping somebody would hear. I don't know how long I screamed, whether for minutes or hours, but suddenly I felt large hands on my shoulder. The hands were pulling me away from Mom, and I tried to hold on even tighter.

"No, Mom, no!" I screamed, opening my eyes and hoping she was still alive.

The large hands belonged to my father, and when I saw his warm welcome face I loosened my grip. There was fear in his eyes, and he looked much older than I'd ever seen him look before. He stroked my head twice, then rose to his full height and took Mom in his arms. He stood there for several long minutes, holding her and telling her everything would be OK.

I sat frozen on the floor, hugging my knees to my chest as he pulled the rope off the rafters. It fell to my feet like a coiled snake, and I instinctively covered my face with my hands. Through my fingers I watched him then gently lead Mom toward the door and up the stairs.

Only when they were gone did I get up and follow the tracks of her tears, which led all the way back to her bedroom. When I got there, the door was closed. I knew it was shut for a reason, so I didn't go in. Nor did I ever mention the incident to anybody, just as nobody said anything about it to me. It was several days later before I saw my mother again, and by then she was back to normal and smiling at me as if nothing had happened.

I tried my best to cope in school, but it seemed meaningless when the rest of my life was in shambles. Nothing seemed more ridiculous at the time than having to make an apron in home economics class. I didn't know how to sew, and I didn't care to learn. The project, painful in its own way, was a disaster almost from the start.

The teacher gave each student a swath of flowered fabric, out of which we cut the pattern. Then she taught us the basics of working the sewing machine. As she talked, we were to stitch the fabric. I did my best to concentrate, but it was impossible to watch her lips and feed the cloth through the machine at the same time.

Two weeks into the project, as I was stitching the pocket, I glanced up at the teacher. Moments later I felt a sharp jab of pain in my thumb. I screamed and jerked my hand back, only to discover my thumb was impaled upon the needle of the machine.

As my blood beaded around the needle and ran onto the fabric, tears welled in my eyes. I looked around for help, but others around me were laughing and pointing. The teacher ran to my side, pulled my thumb off the needle and sent me to the nurse. I survived the accident, but it ruined my attitude toward sewing. My apron remained unfinished after six weeks, and I got a *D* in the course, as I did in most of my other classes.

My mother had a second brush with death shortly after Dad's sister and her husband died in a Youngstown car accident. Nobody called to tell my father; he heard it on the eleven o'clock news. Though he and Mom went to the funeral together, she ran for her bedroom afterward and refused to come out.

Several days later I saw her bedroom door was open, and so I stepped inside. I called her name, but she was nowhere to be found. I began looking elsewhere for her, but when she didn't turn up I enlisted my father's help. The longer we looked, the more anxious we both became. I chased after him as he sprinted from room to room, throwing open every closet and looking beneath every bed.

I followed as he dashed outside, calling her name again and again as the sun was setting. I pointed to the detached garage, which was closed, and Dad suddenly told me to go back in the house. But I stayed where I was as he darted to the garage door and lifted it in one quick motion. He stepped inside through a fog of gray smoke, and I began to tremble.

Afraid to go any closer, I watched as he reached through the open windows of our car, shut the ignition off, and dropped the keys into his shirt pocket. The tail-pipe immediately stopped belching exhaust, and I stood there shaking as I watched him lean down to Mom and begin talking with her. Then he slowly helped her out of the car.

She seemed unsteady as she stood there in her terry slippers and pink, short-sleeved robe, so he held her arm and helped her walk. As the two of them passed by, Dad looked down at me. With a slight nod of his head, he said, "She's OK." But I knew she wasn't, not really.

A few months later Mom attempted suicide again. I'd wandered into her room to talk but found her sound asleep in bed. I tried to shake her awake. I shook her and shook her but got no response. Fearing the worst, I ran screaming through the house for my father. He came running, as did my brother Bobby.

Spotting a near-empty prescription bottle on the bathroom floor, Bobby sprinted for the phone. I stayed in the doorway, watching as my father picked up Mom's hand and began whispering in her ear.

When her eyes eventually opened, I breathed a sigh of relief. And then as he told her an ambulance had been summoned, she suddenly became wide awake. She insisted she really hadn't taken that many pills and would be fine.

Dad just nodded with a warm, compassionate smile. "Yes, dear, you'll be fine," he said. "You'll be fine."

With those major fault lines splitting my family and home wide open, I entered Boardman High. Having no roots outside my disintegrating home life, I joined a campus social club. I found acceptance in that group, which became a surrogate family. To them, my deafness didn't seem to matter.

Of all the group members, Mary Beth was the most friendly. Snow white with long, straight hair, she was several years older and adopted me like a sister. Due to our age difference, she had her own friends, but she always waved when we saw each other at school and picked me up for the Saturday morning meetings and outside functions.

She eventually encouraged me to run for various appointed offices in the group. To be elected, I had to memorize long ritualistic statements, which Mary Beth volunteered to help me with. She left notes on my locker—sometimes "Just to say hi" or else to tell me where to meet after school to go over the memorization. Often we met by the ticket gate at the football field, which was along the route I walked home. Sometimes we stopped by her house, which I liked because her parents were never home, and she made us a treat of hamburgers and fries.

One Friday of my freshman year, Mary Beth asked me to sleep over at her home. We stayed up late talking, and then crawled into a pair of twin beds in her brother's room. She said he was away at college.

Just as I was about to go to sleep, I felt something bump my bed and opened my eyes. In the dim glow of the nightlight, I saw Mary Beth standing there looking down at me. She had a funny look in her eyes which I hadn't seen before. Slowly, very slowly she stretched out her hand and touched my head and gently stroked my hair. And then she leaned down and kissed me. It was a soft, tender kiss unlike I had ever experienced before.

Mary Beth drew back slightly and looked at me again. When I didn't do or say anything, she motioned me to move over. I slid up against the wall and felt her warm body slip under the covers beside me. When her hand touched me, I lay perfectly still. I didn't move. I didn't fight it. For the first time in a very long time I felt warm and secure. Uncle Keith's hands grabbed and demanded. Hers were soft. I'd never had a friend like Mary Beth and didn't want to lose her.

With Mary Beth's assistance, I was able to move up through the ranks of the group and was eventually named the state organist. In that role I played for special functions throughout Ohio, including the week-long state convention, attended by three thousand other high school girls.

I knew nobody when I arrived at the convention. That first evening, as I stood in the dinner line, the girl in front of me turned around and said, "Have you heard about this year's organist?"

"What about her?" I shrugged innocently.

"She's deaf."

"Gee, I didn't know that," I said, wondering what else she might have heard.

"Deaf as a doornail," she assured me. "Not only that, but she's blind too!"

"No fooling—blind as a bat?"

"No fooling."

Later that night, I played a piano solo in the convention hall. At the end of the song, I promptly left the stage. But a woman backstage quickly steered me back out. What I saw surprised me. Three thousand students were on their feet, applauding wildly. Though I couldn't hear the applause, I felt the vibrations. And the vibrations gave me goose bumps from head to toe.

Afterward, the girl I'd met in the dinner line rushed up to me. "I feel so stupid," she said, her face red with embarrassment. "But that's what I was told. Everybody said the organist was blind and deaf."

"No, just deaf," I said. "Deaf as a doornail, but happy as a lark."

Back in Boardman, I stopped by Mary Beth's house almost every day after school. Even after she graduated, she waited for me near the campus, and we would walk to her home together, fix hamburgers, and then go into her room and close the door.

One night after dinner, my parents approached me. They said one of my teachers had called to say my relationship with Mary Beth didn't look right.

"Look right?" I asked, my heart racing.

"The teacher says you're spending too much time together. She's much older than you, and people are talking," Mom said.

I looked at her coldly. Then I looked away at the wall, unwilling to watch her lips. I knew what she wanted. She wanted me to say I would never see Mary Beth again. But how could she, of all people, ask that after leaving my life in emotional rubble herself? Didn't Mom know she'd been the mortar holding my life together, only for it to disintegrate into powder and dust when she'd tried to take her life?

Who was she to talk? I could no longer take her advice. And I refused to heed my father's. Never before had I willfully disobeyed them in such a major way. Had I known that my disobedience would eventually lead to long, painful years of on-again, off-again homosexuality, I would have done what they said. But I knew none of that. All I knew was that Mary Beth had lifted me out of the rubble, and I wasn't about to give her up.

Still, they kept insisting that I end the relationship. She was too old. People were talking. Over and over they said it. I wondered what people were saying and how much my parents knew. The more I thought about it, the more tired and tense I got. If I quit seeing her, I would be alone.

The thought of that gave me splitting headaches, and one day I asked a teacher for a pass to the nurse's office. The nurse gave me two aspirin and let me lie down.

When the period ended, I pretended I was asleep. I didn't want to go to class. I was failing my courses. Even though I sat in the front rows, I couldn't read the teacher's lips and take notes at the same time. Even though I saw the questions asked by the teacher, I never heard the answers given.

The nurse shook me lightly, but when I didn't respond, she shook me harder. My eyes remained closed. I was tired of just sitting in class, understanding only bits and pieces. I felt disconnected. Alone. Nobody wanted me to have a friend. I knew the relationship was wrong, but there was much about it that was right. Mary Beth and I could talk and joke and laugh together. She had time for me. When I was with her, I felt cared for and loved. I felt I *mattered* to her. And I knew I didn't matter to anybody else in my next class or to the teacher or to anybody in the class after that. And so I kept my eyes closed as she shook and shook me.

About ten minutes later, with my eyes still closed, I felt myself being lifted. I was placed onto what seemed like a bed with wheels, and a strap was placed over me. Then I was rolled somewhere. Out the door? It was suddenly brighter, so I had to be outdoors. But I wasn't sure where, and I didn't really want to look.

I then felt bumpy, uneven movement as the bed was lifted and slid forward, followed by a *whump!* of a closing car door. Then we were moving, and waves of vibrations rolled over my body as if I were standing beside a pipe organ playing at full tilt. The bones of my body, all of them, were reverberating—fast vibrations quite unlike those of the car itself. Who was I with, and where was I being taken?

Slowly, very slowly, I relaxed my eyelids and lifted them a very small fraction of a crack. A glimmer of light fused through my eyelashes, but it was like I was looking through a blanket. I still couldn't tell where I was. I lifted them a bit more, slowly, almost imperceptibly. In the diffused light I finally saw that I wasn't in a car at all, but in some sort of truck or van that was filled with a pulsing red light. I raised my eyes slightly more.

My heart jumped when I finally realized where I was. I was in an ambulance! The vibrations had to be from the siren. That also explained the red light and . . . *What was that?* I felt cold instruments on my body. A stethoscope? I hoped. But my mind imagined that maybe they—whoever *they* were—thought I was dead and would use heart paddles to jump-start me awake.

Then I really got scared. I thought of the TV cop shows where paramedics jolted accident victims back to life. Maybe they would try to do the same to me. I only hoped they felt my heart beating as much as I did. It was lurching in my chest, and if they had good ears they could probably *hear* it.

I shut my eyes tight and hoped the bad dream would pass. My mind reeled with fears about what would happen at the hospital. For all I knew, the doctors would decide something was wrong inside my head and perform emergency brain surgery. I wanted to open my eyes and tell everybody it was all a mistake; that I just had a small headache and didn't want to go to class. But I didn't. I just lay there like a corpse—like Mom the day she wouldn't wake up.

When the ambulance lurched to a halt, I was whisked out and rolled away. My nostrils filled with a sudden antiseptic smell, and I knew I was in the hospital. I also realized I would be in big trouble if I carried my ruse any further. I knew somebody had probably contacted my mother, and I couldn't begin to imagine her reaction.

The bed was still rolling when I finally decided to open my eyes. Moments later, everybody around me realized my eyes were open and swarmed around me, sticking their faces close to mine and smiling warmly and asking me if I was OK and if I had any memory of what had just happened. Everybody's lips were moving at once, and I looked back and forth trying to sort them out. Finally I focused on the lips of one, a doctor.

"Yes, I feel fine," I said. "No, I don't have a headache," I continued in response to his questions. Then I lied. "The last thing I remember was getting two aspirin and lying down. I think I just fell asleep."

For the next several hours, I was examined head to toe, X-rayed, and given a brain scan. Nothing turned up, and I kept insisting I felt fine. Still they probed and prodded. When I was finally taken to a room and allowed to see my parents, they rushed to my side and held me. Mom had tears in her eyes.

"My little Susie," she cried.

"Mom, I'm fine. Really, nothing is wrong."

"We brought you some flowers," my father said, pointing to a vase of roses on the bedstand.

"Thank you," I said, smiling. "Can we take them and go home now?"

"We'll see," Mom said. "Not all the lab reports are in yet, and the doctors want you here so they can monitor your progress."

"But—"

"Just be patient," my father said.

"They don't know exactly what happened or why, but they're concerned about your face," Mom noted.

"What about my face?"

"Oh, nothing," she said.

"What about my face?"

"I shouldn't have said anything."

"What's the matter with my face?"

"Well," she began, glancing at my father, then back to me. I read the hesitancy on her lips and in her eyes. "They say one side of your mouth, the right side, is crooked. It's drooping more than the other side."

"No, that's silly," I said, unable to believe medical experts could be so easily fooled. "I feel fine and want to go home now. Nothing is wrong with my face, and nothing is drooping."

"Why don't you just rest awhile," Mom said, ignoring my comments. She ran her fingers through my hair and bent down to kiss me on the forehead.

In the moment her face neared my own, I saw the little wrinkles around her eyes. She looked desperate and vulnerable and very human. I felt convinced that her attempts on her life were for attention, just like my little fainting spell was. The attention suddenly showered upon me felt good, as it must have for her. But with every warm smile and query of concern, I felt a profound sense of shame. I was a fake, a first-class phony.

Perhaps even worse was the realization that I was a desperate human being—just like my mother. We were not so unlike after all. My mind flashed back to scenes of her noose and gassy garage and empty bottle of pills.

Granted, her cries for attention were louder and more dramatic than my own, but for the first time I understood how she probably had felt. She undoubtedly felt just like me, which wasn't a good way to feel at all.

And so, with tears in my eyes, I wrapped my arms around her neck and pulled her close. When I let go, she looked at me in the gentle kind of way I remembered as a child.

"What are you crying about?" she asked.

"Oh, nothing," I said. And then I gave her another hug and didn't want to let go.

10

COLLEGE BOUND

espite failing many of my classes, I was promoted each year to the next grade. Teachers just pushed me ahead, perhaps because they didn't want me two years in a row. Most of my courses were in business, which was my high school's equivalent of the Dummy Class. I was supposed to learn to be a good secretary, but shorthand got in the way. Having only one set of eyes, I couldn't read lips and write accurately at the same time. Consequently, my shorthand was worse than bad and looked like a combination of chicken scratches and hieroglyphics. I flunked that course too.

Most of my learning, therefore, was from outside tutors such as Miss Martin, who taught me to love books. Books became my ears, and from them I learned about ideas and people and a world that was bigger than the one I knew in my little Boardman, Ohio.

I had one high school teacher who was different from all the others, however. She believed in me despite what my report cards showed. At times, she even believed in me more than I did myself. Her name was Georgiana Parker, and she taught typing.

Barely five feet tall with hair the color of concrete, Miss Parker wore two-piece suits when dresses were in style and was as abrupt as a whirlwind. When she passed by, I squirmed in my seat as if a time bomb were about to go off. But she did her job and, after three years, told me my typing sounded like falling rain. I didn't know what she meant but took it as a compliment.

No matter how fast or well I typed, she always demanded more. "You probably don't realize it now, but typing will open many doors for you," she told me one day. "So work hard and be prepared. If all else fails, you can always fall back on typing."

Miss Parker also recognized something in me that other teachers didn't. She took my ability to type 127 words per minute as a sign of intelligence. In her eyes I was no dummy. She was even audacious enough to suggest I might have college potential.

"What do you want to do after you graduate?" she asked me one day after class. "Do you want to go to college?"

I wanted to be like hearing kids, and they were going to college. But I knew there were many barriers. Due to my low grades I couldn't take college preparatory classes, and I knew I couldn't get into college just because I typed fast.

As if reading my thoughts, she said, "I know you've got some strikes against you. But the worst thing that can happen is for the college to say no. I'll do what I can to help them say yes."

Miss Parker arranged to have my IQ tested, and as she suspected, the results indicated I had above-average intelligence. She also informed me that residents of Ohio were guaranteed the opportunity to attend a state university for at least two semesters.

Upon graduation from Boardman High with a *D*-plus grade point average, I finally received my acceptance notice from Ohio State University in Columbus. My parents promptly threw a party for friends and neighbors on my behalf. Emblazoned across the top of the sheet cake, frosted with the scarlet and gray university colors, were these words:

> *Congratulations, Sue.*
> *College bound—Ohio State.*

Preparations to leave for college took almost a month. My parents bought a metal footlocker, which I packed and repacked with new clothes, sheets, towels, stationery supplies, together with all of my hopes and dreams.

I'd never left home before for any length of time, so the approach of the parting was traumatic and tearful. The summer before I left, Mom and I fought like tigers. She knew what I didn't: once I left, I probably wouldn't return home.

Her nerves were tauter than tightropes, and she had several spells that last summer. The closer my departure, the more intense and frequent our arguments became. Our disputes were often about relatively insignificant issues. I wanted to stay out late and wear blue jeans; she preferred me in dresses and home early. The real issue, of course, was that I no longer was her little Susie who was entirely dependent on her.

"Lower your voice; I don't want the neighbors to hear," Mom said during one heated argument.

I promptly stomped into my bedroom, threw open my window, and screamed at the top of my lungs, "I don't care who hears this!"

Upon arriving at Ohio State, I was met at my cramped dorm in Brown Hall by my new roommate, a girl who was short and stout, with thinning brown hair that hinted at baldness. When I walked in, she eyed me skeptically from behind a thick pair of glasses. I sensed an immediate and immense dislike. The strain continued for several days until I could stand it no longer. I finally approached her and looked her square in the eyes.

"You don't like me, do you?" I said.

"That's right."

"You haven't liked me from day one."

"That's right."

"Why?"

"I don't know."

I didn't know either, but I wasn't about to stick around and find out. The air was so thick between us that I switched rooms. My new roommates were more accepting but disapproved of my life-style. I didn't smoke marijuana. They quickly corrected that and, in addition, introduced me to a diet of pizza and beer. Most weekends I ended up on High Street, which had more bars than a dog has fleas and swarmed with a large percentage of the 42,000 students attending Ohio State. During my freshman year, the Buckeye football team was on a four-year championship roll, and after Saturday afternoon wins I joined thousands of other students on all-night drinking binges along High Street, which was so crowded that police closed it off to week-end traffic.

The post-football game scene was a blur of drunken enthusiasm in which everybody loved everybody, and if you ran out of liquor there were dozens of people who would gladly offer you a swig from their bottle. Kegs lined the sidewalk, and policemen interfered with nothing other than to ensure that partygoing didn't erupt into open fighting or public sex.

By getting plastered at High Street parties, I no longer felt isolated and lonely. There was action and movement and hugging, and I felt very much a part of the hearing world, even though it was impossible for me to read lips when drunk. I guzzled Stroh's beer by the pitcher, reveling with the attention I got by outdrinking my companions.

The girls were no competition. My biggest thrill was beating the guys. We drank boilermakers—beer topped by a shot of whiskey—until all but one of the competitors toppled over. I was always the last on my feet and would signal my win by wiping the beer from my mouth with the back of my hand and letting loose a horrific belch that made everybody roar.

While sex didn't occur in the middle of High Street, it was practiced almost as openly. Living a few doors down from me was a coed whose goal was to bed down every first-string football player at the university. Most nights at about ten thirty, she slipped down the back stairs dressed to kill, returning a few minutes later with one Buckeye player or another. He would stay until the following morning. People called her the hooker of

Brown Hall, which always saddened me because despite her undercover pursuits, I saw in her a loneliness—like my own—that nothing and no one could fill.

When sober, I was enthralled with being at college—the stately beauty of the campus, the security of the old buildings, the challenge of independence, the inspiration of the library. Just walking across the campus made me feel like I was a brilliant Ph.D. I wanted to study, to better myself, to lift my sights and goals, to become something more than I was. The reality, however, was that I was flunking every single class my first semester.

Though I sat in the front row of each class, I was lost amidst the two hundred-plus students. I followed only a small fraction of each lecture because the professors seldom stood still. Many spoke from the blackboard with their back turned, or from the side of their mouth while clenching a pipe in their teeth. Others had bushy beards and mustaches, which covered their lips. When a professor asked a question, I was worse off than in elementary school. Turning around in my seat, I stared at a sea of faces, trying to figure out who was speaking and what the answer was. Getting nothing out of class, I tried to rely on the assigned books but found the tests were primarily based on lecture material. So I finally quit going to class and studying, and spent my time on High Street instead.

At the end of the semester, I felt depressed and alone. Walking out of one of my classes with my head hanging, I rounded a corner and ran smack into a blind student. His books and notes were scattered on the walkway, and as I stooped to pick them up I wondered how a blind student could take such copious notes.

We got talking, and as it turned out, he was the brother of one of the girls in my dorm. Later I told him I wouldn't be at Ohio State much longer because of my failing grades.

"Who's taking notes for you?" he asked.

"Notes?"

"You must have somebody helping you with class notes."

"No, I don't know what you're talking about."

"Maybe that's why you're flunking out," he said. "In my classes, I have people who give me their notes. You should look into it."

"I don't know anybody or talk to anybody in my classes. I don't even know when the prof calls my name. I just go in at the start of class and walk out at the end."

"Give me your schedule for next semester, and I'll talk to my sister," he said. "We'll work on a plan."

The following week, he called to say they had arranged note takers for each of my courses. When I later received my first set of notes, I couldn't believe what I had been missing. I pored over the notes in each of my classes, studying them all night before a test.

I could barely contain my excitement when I took my first test under the new system. I looked down at the question sheet and was amazed to see the very things I had read in my notes. It was a major revelation that students could know, merely by studying notes of what the professor said in class, exactly what would be on the test! In quick order, my test results jumped to *C*s and *B*s, boosting my grade point average high enough to enable me to remain at Ohio State.

I was fortunate that my college bills for tuition, books, and room and board were covered by vocational rehabilitation, a state program to help educate handicapped people and provide them with saleable skills. Without outside aid, my parents could not have afforded to send me to college.

Not wanting me to rely solely on handouts, Mom picked up part-time jobs for the first time since she was married, sending me the majority of each paycheck for pocket money. Her first job was distributing free food samples in grocery stores; later she clerked in a gift shop. The income she turned over to me was a sacrificial gift, and to my shame I squandered it on High Street.

My weight ballooned accordingly, which caused me great anguish. Dad jokingly referred to me as the halfback for the Cleveland Browns, but I could see the pain in his eyes when I traveled home for vacations and long weekends. At my peak of three hundred and plenty pounds, I dwarfed his rail-thin body. I know he agonized about the disappearance of his little Susie, the skating wunderkind who held crowds spellbound with her aerial spins and jumps.

My weight problem also caused distress because I loved to play racquetball, golf, swim, and go on long, fast walks. But that wasn't possible when I felt as if I were lugging around two other people on my back. I knew I stuck out like a sore thumb around those who were physically fit, and I cringed to see their stares and comments.

Desperately wanting to fit in, I became the life of all the parties, getting so drunk and loaded on drugs that I could barely stand. People laughed, but I knew they were laughing at me. They wanted me at the parties because I was good entertainment. Several nights, I felt so empty afterward that I went on a screaming, crying rampage when I got back to my room. I tore posters off my wall, knocked books onto the floor, and ripped up index cards on which I'd written inspirational quotations. Previously, the sayings had encouraged me when nobody else was around. They inspired me to keep going when times were hard, to maintain hope when I was despairing. But at my lowest, blackest moments, they seemed to mock me with their false hope and exclamatory optimism.

After destroying them, the mess littered the floor for several days—until I finally got down on my hands and knees, pieced and taped the jigsaw fragments together, and pinned them back to the wall, where they remained only until my next tantrum.

The day after one such outburst, I accidentally smashed my head on the bunk bed. Concerned about their own schedules and schoolwork and problems, other students hardly noticed I'd been injured. I began crying, and then crying harder and harder. Tears flowed as if from a faucet. I felt so desperately lonely.

Deep in my heart I knew the truth. I was crying for attention more than from pain. But so what? I was tired of being on the outside, looking in on the hearing world, yet it was obvious nobody really cared about me and my needs. A thought rifled through my mind, and I tried to shake it off. I was afraid of what I'd do to find acceptance.

Still, nobody came. And so I acted on the thought, getting attention the only sure way I knew how.

I suddenly threw myself on the floor and began shaking violently. As my body bucked against the cold linoleum and my arms and legs shook and twitched like a disjointed marionette, students came running.

I could only imagine what they were saying:

"Sue! Something's wrong with Sue!" somebody would shout.

"I think she bumped her head."

"Oh, God, look at her!"

"She's having a seizure!"

"Quick, somebody call an ambulance!"

I glared out with a wild panicked eye, grunting incoherently through my clenched teeth. When an ambulance eventually did arrive, attendants slipped a blanket beneath my head to keep me from cracking my skull, which I wasn't about to do. I rolled my eyes back and went rigid. My arms and legs trembled, and then I gave a huge grunt and went limp. My eyes focused again and I looked groggily about as if I were Dorothy who'd just awaken after her dreamy adventure in Oz. Dozens of faces were gathered about.

"What's everybody staring at?" I asked innocently.

"You've just had a convulsive seizure," the lips of one attendant said.

"When?"

"Moments ago."

"I don't remember," I said.

"That's not uncommon."

"Where are you taking me?" I asked as they lifted me onto a portable gurney.

"OSU Hospital."

On the way to the hospital, I acted as if I wanted to do nothing but sleep. When we arrived, I was guided to my room and given Valium, phenobarbital and Dilantin capsules. As the drugs coursed through my body, I felt a sudden release, as if I didn't have a concern in the world.

"How are you feeling now?" a nurse asked.

"Yes," I said drunkenly. "Yes . . . yes . . . *yes!*" My arms were as lifeless as a rag doll's, and I could not keep my eyes open. The nurse disappeared somewhere, and I turned over in bed and slept long and hard.

When I woke up, the nurses looked like monsters. Their heads were swollen, and the walls were moving in and out like giant lungs. The hallucinations continued for several hours, and then everything returned to normal. From that point on, I refused to take any more drugs.

For two days, I was monitored around the clock, and I was even given an electroencephalogram to measure the electrical activity in my brain. To my utter astonishment, the light on the machine blinked red at one point and the needle on the graph paper jumped.

"What's that?" I asked, turning to face a pair of doctors and a nurse at my side. I was careful not to dislodge the tiny needles that had been inserted into my scalp at various points. They were so small they didn't hurt, but I knew they could easily be disconnected.

"The light flashes when we encounter scar tissue," one of the doctors said.

"Scar tissue from what?"

"The seizures."

"I don't get it," I said.

"Careful of the leads," the nurse said, placing a calming hand on my shoulder. She wanted me to turn around, but I kept my eyes fixed on the doctor's lips.

"The EEG detects damage from a seizure," he said. "It's nothing major in most cases, and with yours there appears to be just a single spot of inactivity. A very small bit of scar tissue. Certainly nothing to be concerned about."

"From the seizure?" I asked again, dumfounded that I had fooled both the doctors *and* their expensive machine. If there was any hint of scar tissue, I figured it was probably from getting beaned in the head as a kid by a well-aimed crab apple, or from smashing into the bunk bed earlier.

"Yes, yes of course," he replied, as I stared at him in disbelief and shock.

When I was released from the hospital, I was given a prescription for muscle relaxants. I stockpiled the medication, though for what I didn't know. It wasn't long before I discovered a good reason. One night after a party, I returned to my room feeling down and depressed. I was tired of living on the planet, of going through all the motions of life but not really living or understanding. I wanted to self-destruct.

I downed a handful of pills and then lay down in bed and waited. Deep inside, I wanted somebody to burst through the door and hold me in their arms and tell me they loved me and that everything would be all right.

I thought of how I had once held onto Mom, pleading with her not to hang herself, and how my father had come running when he heard me screaming for help. But nobody heard my cries now. Even if they had, I would never have known because I couldn't hear so much as a knock on the door. When nobody came, I cried out to God, asking him to remove the emptiness in my life and help me hang on.

The more I waited, the more I thought of the sacrifices my parents had made to enable me to get as far as I had. Despite our many differences, I knew they loved me. I didn't want to hurt them, and I didn't want to be separated from God for eternity.

As the drugs entered my bloodstream, my body was so relaxed that I didn't know if I had the strength to sit up. Finally I pulled myself up by the windowsill. Outside the night was dark, but the sky was lit by billions of stars. All was calm, all was bright. I remembered my song, "Silent Night," and began to sing. The more I sang, the more I knew I was not ready to die. There was still hope.

With every ounce of willpower I had left, I stumbled out of bed and groped toward the room of my dorm advisor. The next thing I knew, I was in the hospital, coughing and fighting as a suction tube was inserted through my nose and down into my stomach.

I was taken back to my dorm room to convalesce, but for days the desperate ache would not go away. I lay in bed unable to move and unwilling to talk with others. And then in the stillness of my rampaged room, I pulled an old Bible from my trunk—a Bible that had previously gathered dust at home and which I'd packed almost as an afterthought. I flipped it open and began to read.

I didn't understand everything. There were strange customs and odd ideas. Thousands of years separated the time when the words were written and when I read them. One verse in particular seemed to jump off the page: "Come unto me, all ye that labor and are heavy laden, and I will give you rest" (Matthew 11:28). Across the centuries, the words filled me with a sense of comfort that I'd been missing. I knew I was weary. I was burdened. And I desperately needed to find rest for my soul. I needed a lasting peace that could not come from another person, a peace that could only be heaven-sent.

I eventually decided that I couldn't feel loved as long as I looked and felt like a blimp. And so one day I bought a pair of athletic shoes and went on a very slow four-mile walk. It was a time of drawing close with God, thinking things through, readjusting my priorities, and again determining that my health was truly important. Along the way, I prayed and asked God to help me feel loveable and change my life.

I walked twice a day, working against a clock. As my weight came off, I picked up my pace, walking faster and faster until I could eventually jog the distance. Losing weight was no easy task. I had to drastically alter my habits and life-style, but for the first time I felt a desire to do that. I ate mostly vegetables and quit boozing. The diet was like detoxification, and my head throbbed for weeks. When I ran, I sometimes felt like I was dying. But I kept up my regimen, working as if in training for a championship meet.

The pain was compensated by the thrill of seeing the needle of the scale go down. When I hit 135 pounds, it was the best feeling in the world. Nobody handed me a trophy. Nobody cheered from the sidelines. I did it myself—with a little help from above.

With that goal attained, and feeling better about myself, I felt ready to take the next step, wherever it led.

11

MAKING PEACE

During my second year at Ohio State, Vietnam War protests rocked the campus, and the shooting of student demonstrators at nearby Kent State created aftershocks that threatened to shut down the university. The friction hit home one day as I was returning to my dorm. Sudden chaos broke out around me.

Everybody was running, glancing back over their shoulders with fear and hate in their eyes. Some stopped to yell, but I was not close enough to see what they were screaming about. People I didn't know sprinted past me. Some ducked into my hall and darted up the stairs. Others dashed in the front door and slipped out the back. I picked up my pace and then began to run.

The air was filled with something stringent and stinging. I wiped my eyes and tried to run faster. Students swarmed around me in a mad frenzy. Uncontrollable tears streamed down my face. I looked back. What I saw made my heart pound. Moving down the street toward me was the National Guard. They were dressed in green fatigues, like those I saw nightly on television. As they approached, I saw them lobbing tear gas canisters at clusters of students.

Then I really began to run, sprinting across the lawn of my building, taking the steps in two strides, and then blasting through the front doors and up the steps toward my room. On the way I bumped against dozens of unfamiliar students who were filing into the basement with wet rags held over their mouths and noses.

As I raced down the hallway, somebody grabbed me from behind and stuck a wet bandanna and a pair of binoculars in my hands. I was surrounded by several people I'd met at various parties who'd been amused with stories I told about lipreading.

At those parties, I'd told them about how in restaurants I sometimes "eavesdropped" on conversations around me. One night I noticed a lone woman sitting nearby. As she was finishing her meal, a man slipped into a chair beside her. My eyes bulged when I realized he was trying to pick her up and take her back to his motel room. At first the conversation was humorous, but when it turned trashy I felt my face flush and my ears burn with embarrassment.

I'd related that I'd seen a lot of very bad language from a distance, but none worse than from football coaches on television after their team missed a key play or the referee made a bad call. I'd also told them how much I enjoyed baseball games when the camera zoomed in on players conversing in the dugout, or on the manager when he walked out to the mound to talk with a troubled pitcher. The most animated and unrepeatable conversations occurred when the manager stormed to the plate and went nose-to-nose with the umpire.

However, nobody was laughing now. They were all talking at once and steering me to the front of our building, toward the giant glass windows that overlooked the entire street. Their eyes were all bloodshot from the gas, and those with bandannas on their faces looked like western bandits from old cowboy-and-Indian movies.

"What's going on?" I demanded, stopping in my tracks. Others pushed me from behind to keep me moving. Their lips moved so fast I couldn't keep up.

". . . the pigs . . . ," snarled one pair of lips.

". . . headed our way . . . ," came another.

". . . the binoculars . . ."

". . . by reading their lips, you can . . ."

". . . and tell us what they're saying . . ."

". . . other areas of campus, but first we must . . ."

". . . stay low and out of sight . . ."

"Hold it!" I said. "I'm only getting parts of what everybody's saying. Somebody give it to me straight and slow. What's going on, and what am I doing holding these field glasses?"

"We've gotta move fast," said a girl who lived a few doors down. "The pigs are on top of us, and reports say they're storming the campus. We don't know where they're headed next. That's why we need you, and that's what the binoculars are for. We thought maybe you could read the pigs' lips and tell us what they're saying and . . . well, maybe you can figure out where they're headed, and we can alert people there to evacuate."

"Very good," I said. "Let's go."

Perched against the windowsill with the binoculars glued to the glass, I scanned the approaching National Guard members until I spotted somebody who looked like he was in charge. He lagged behind the foot patrol and held a bullhorn to his lips. I wiped my teary, stinging eyes and peered hard through the glasses.

"OK, I'm on target," I said to no one in particular. I focused the glasses as the group moved closer. "But his lips are covered. I don't know what he's saying. I can't make out . . . wait . . . he's looking at a map. Now he's talking into the bullhorn again and scratching his head. He's saying something, but I don't . . . no, he's cussing up a storm and pointing and looking at the map and now he's . . . *north to Townsend Hall,* I caught that much. That much was clear, he said, *'north to Townsend Hall,'* and now he's pointing again and talking into the bullhorn, and I think they're headed that way! They're cutting across to Townsend!"

I glanced up at the ring of students around me and two of them dashed for the phone to alert those at the nearby dorm to evacuate.

The experience at the time was very real and frightening, prompting in me a significant amount of soul-searching and questioning about the meaning of life and purpose of authority. In my mind, authority that clubbed and gassed students was bad authority. By preventing somebody from getting his head split open, I felt I was, in a small way, helping to restore sensibility and stop a bad war. I was a peacemaker.

In my mind, nothing justified Vietnam. I couldn't understand why young men my age were sent there, or why students at Kent State lost their lives protesting them being sent. *Why?* Those were truly mixed-up times, and I often tried to make sense of them beneath the shade of a firmly rooted buckeye in The Oval. The Oval was a quiet, worry-free place, nestled amidst the majestic trees, bell tower, and ivy-covered campus buildings that had been around since the beginning of time. I went there between classes and often on Saturdays, cooling my bare feet in the grass and watching people saunter along the zig-zagging sidewalks that dissected the green expanse. But the pathways were suddenly emptied one day when The Oval was clouded by tear gas and taken over by the National Guard.

Unable to go there, I began scouting the campus for a church—a hideaway where I could think and feel safe and not have to worry about war and faraway places. I tried the doors of Methodist, Lutheran, and Baptist churches, but they were locked except on Sundays. Only the doors of the Catholic church remained unlocked twenty-four hours a day, so that's where I went.

The chapel was small and rather dark, with a large wooden crucifix hanging above the altar. I had never been inside a Catholic church before, and on my early visits I felt uneasy, like I did as a child when friends of my parents stopped by and I was seated in a stiff-backed chair and told to be seen, not heard. The real uneasiness came from remembering how Mom treated my brother for marrying a Catholic girl. She made it very clear that Catholicism was for other people and would not be tolerated in our home.

I also found it awkward the first time I went to a Sunday Mass. I didn't know what to do. I sat in the last row, and when the people stood up, I stood up. When they sat down, I sat down. When they kneeled, I kneeled. After a few services, I got the rhythm down; after a few more, I began to see the beauty in the repetition of liturgies and the lighting of candles. The more I returned, the more peaceful and serene I felt.

The church was my haven, a quiet spot where I could be alone to pray and think through God's direction of my life. I began going several days a week in the off hours, sitting in a front pew where I kneeled before the magnificent cross. During those periods, I often wondered and prayed about my lost brother, Billy. The more I wondered, the more I prayed; the more I prayed, the more I wondered. Finally, I realized I had no choice but to track him down. I wanted to ask his side of the story.

During my next Thanksgiving semester break, I went home and searched through the local phone book. In Youngstown there were many Thomases listed; eight had William as first names. Looking closer, I discovered one William H. Thomas, Jr. My heart raced as I copied down the address, which was within five minutes of my parents' house.

I drove over unannounced the next evening after dinner. I pulled to the curb, fronting a neat Cape Cod home. I double-checked the address with that on my piece of paper and then walked up the drive. I took several deep breaths to clear my mind and knocked twice on the door. Two fast, solid knocks.

My brother answered. I'd not seen him since our awkward meeting at my grandmother's funeral. He looked the same as he had then and much the same as I remembered him from before he left, except for his waist and thinning hair. I doubted, however, that he had any idea who I was.

"Billy, I'm your sister, Susie," I simply announced.

"I know," he said.

"I didn't call, but I'd like to talk with you."

"Do you want to come in?"

"Yeah, sure."

Inside, his wife, Barbara, shook my hand and steered me into the living room, which she kept as immaculate as Mom's. Barbara was short and thin, with the open, friendly looks of an Avon lady.

Once seated, I got right to the point. "Billy, I'm old enough now that I'd like to hear your side of the story," I began. "I was always told you ran away from home, that you didn't love us anymore. If that's true, all I want to know is why?"

Billy shook his head. "I didn't run away. I was kicked out."

"Mom?"

He nodded. "She asked me to leave because I was engaged to Barbara, who was a Catholic. One day she just told me to pack my things and get out."

"How about Dad?"

"He was mad. Didn't think I showed enough respect to Mom. They were both against the marriage, and both stood firm in their beliefs."

"I think it all started when your father's first wife died," Barb commented.

"When *who* died?"

"Your dad's first wife."

I stared at her blankly with my mouth agape, wondering what she meant and whether I'd correctly seen what she said.

"You look surprised. You do know—"

"What are you talking about?"

"She doesn't know, Billy."

"What don't I know?"

"That Mom's not my real mom," Billy said. "My real mother died when I was born."

"Nobody ever . . . I never . . . ," I began, but the words wouldn't come. My head suddenly began to spin.

"You OK?" Billy asked.

"This is too much to take in. What you're telling me now is that you're not . . . I mean, you're not *really* my brother," I said.

"Technically your half brother."

I looked at both of them, trying to clear the fog from my head as I wondered why such information had been kept from me all those years. I knew I would never know. "That doesn't change anything," I said quickly. "Half is as good as whole. You're still my brother. But let me ask you. You just said you were kicked out because you were going to marry Barbara. What you don't know is that I have been attending a Catholic church myself."

"Does Mom know?"

I shook my head.

"What are you going to do?"

"I don't know. But I'm not so concerned about the future as with patching up the past so you can come home again. If things could be made right, would you want to come home again?"

"Of course."

"You'd actually do it?"

"Yeah, if Barbara and I were welcome. I'd like my kids to have grandparents."

"OK, Billy, it's going to happen because I'm going to make it happen. After all these years, you're coming home. I won't give up."

I promptly drove home and walked straight up to my parents as they were watching television. "We have to talk," I said, snapping off the set. "I've just come back from talking with Billy, and the story he told me is different from what I've heard from you all my life. He said you kicked him out because of Barbara. I believe that's pretty close to the truth, and I don't want there to be any more separation in our family. Billy wants to come home. So now it's up to you. I'm asking you, will you allow Billy to come home?"

Without warning, Mom burst into tears. "Oh no, no, no! We can't go through this. I will not go through this again!"

I turned my attention to my father. "He's your son. Don't you want him back?"

A distant look glazed his eyes as he nodded his assent. Then he looked at Mom and said, "It's time, Clara. It's been too long. I want my son to come home."

"If it's going to happen, you've got to call him now," I said as Mom cried in her chair. "Not tomorrow, but now."

Dad went to the kitchen where the phone book was sitting on the table. He opened it to the page of Thomases and ran his finger down the columns. When he stopped halfway down, his jaw began to twitch and his eyes brimmed.

"It's the right thing," I said.

As he began to dial, I returned to the living room and sat across from Mom. I looked at her fragile body, wracking with sobs, and said, "I found out something that you or Dad never told me about. I didn't know he was married before or that Billy is my half brother. But I want to tell you something. To me he is my real brother. The 'half' part doesn't matter. The past is history. We can't go on like this anymore."

Later that night I pulled my brother Bobby aside and shared the shock of my discovery with him. "Here I am nineteen years old, and I can't believe I'm the only one who didn't know Dad was married before and that Billy's not our real brother."

Bobby stared at me blankly for several long moments, rose from his seat in slow motion, and walked up to me with a glint in his eyes. Suddenly he balled up his fist and hit me in the shoulder. "You're a liar!"

The shock of his action was stronger than the pain involved. "You mean, you didn't know either?"

"You don't know what you're talking about," he grunted.

"Yes I do, Bobby. Dad's first wife died when Billy was born. He didn't marry Mom until later."

"You're a liar," he repeated, raising his fist again.

I quickly stepped back. "Believe it or not, but it's the truth," I said, rubbing my aching arm as he turned and walked away. "Ask Dad, he'll tell you," I shouted after him.

When Dad hung up the phone with Billy, he announced that an appointment for their visit was set for two weeks later. I had to go back to Ohio State, so I unfortunately missed the homecoming. But Billy told me later I didn't miss much. He said there was an icy fringe on everything and that Mom sat in the living room chair without saying a single word all night.

Nevertheless, Dad invited Billy and Barbara back the following month, and back again after that. Over time, Billy even began stopping by midweek to help Dad blacktop the driveway or fix the roof.

The true miracle, though, was when he showed up on Mother's Day with a bouquet of red roses in his hand. When I heard that, I bawled with joy—the joy of being a peacemaker right in my own home. After years of being kept on the outside, I suddenly felt like I had the inside track. Never had tears felt so good.

Three weeks before finals of my sophomore year, war protests became so vocal that Ohio State shut its doors and sent all the students home to cool off. Even the graduation ceremony was canceled. Through the job placement office at Ohio State, I applied for and was hired to counsel at Camp Newhoca, a mountain retreat for handicapped children outside Hartford, Connecticut.

Before the campers arrived, the counselors all received a week of intense training, trying to get the feel for what it felt like to be truly handicapped. To understand blindness, we spent a day blindfolded. Another day our hands were tied behind our backs, and we took turns feeding and dressing each other.

The campers, ages eight to sixteen, had a wide range of disabilities, including spina bifida, cerebral palsy, and muscular dystrophy. Some were blind or missing critical parts of their body. One of my most vivid memories was working with Roy, a sixteen-year-old who had half a right arm, half a left leg, and no arm or leg on the opposite side. Tall and skinny as a broomstick, he had a mop of blond hair, a crooked smile, and a never-say-die attitude. Though confined to a wheelchair, he knew he could lick the world. And I knew nothing would stop him.

Roy had been coming to the camp for several years but had never swum across the lake, a distance of almost a mile. The summer I worked at the camp, he announced his intention to try. I was the only one who believed he could do it, and he championed his cause until he was finally given permission to attempt the swim. The only provision was that I had to swim beside him, and a rowboat had to follow us.

That very afternoon, I rolled his wheelchair down the dusty trail to the edge of the water. With the aid of two other counselors, I lifted him onto the shore. When I raised a fluorescent orange life jacket to his head, he stepped back.

"Only when I get tired," he said. I could carry it for him just in case.

I nodded, and then strapped one on myself. I knew I'd need all the buoyancy possible if I had to swim for both of us or haul him out of the lake.

"What stroke are you going to use?" I asked as we carried him toward the lake and let him dip the toes of his half leg into the cool, crystal blue water.

"The side stroke!" he beamed through his crooked smile. It was the only stroke he could physically do.

When he was ready, he gave a nod and we turned him loose. Like an undersized fish that is hooked and released, his body movements were initially hesitant, and he stayed close to the shore. But then his half arm began whipping the water, and his short leg kicked from behind. Slowly he began edging away. I stood there in waist-deep water, shaking my head as I watched the gap between us widen from five to ten to fifteen feet. Finally I shoved off and, with a couple of quick strokes, caught up with him.

"Thatta boy, Roy!" I shouted.

On the way across, he grew tired several times, and I draped the life jacket around his neck. We treaded water together until he regained his breath and huffed, "OK, let's go." Then he launched out again, stroking and kicking and lessening the distance to the shore a foot at a time. An hour and a half later, he reached the opposite side. As I moved into position to help him onto the shore to rest, he shook his head, edged around me, and began swimming right back. I could see he was breathing hard, but there was no mistaking his crooked smile. I let him continue.

He went the distance, of course, as I knew he would. When we finally pulled him onto the beach, a swarm of fellow campers and counselors were on hand, cheering and clapping and bursting with pride for one of their own who proved that dreams do come true.

Another precious memory was taking Laura to the archery range. Eleven years old with firecracker spunk, she'd tumbled from a tree as an infant and was paralyzed from the neck down. Since her arms hung limp at her side like broken branches, I held the bow and arrow for her.

With the bow in one hand, I draped my right arm around her slim body and fit a silver-tipped arrow onto the string. As I drew it back, she tucked her head against the bow and told me where to aim. Reading her lips from that angle was difficult, and it didn't help that her hair, which was the orange-red color of campfire coals, whipped in the breeze and obscured my sight.

"To the right," she said. "Not that much . . . back a little . . . down a bit . . . a tad to the left . . . a little more . . . down just a fraction . . . there, perfect—now! Let her rip!"

I held my breath as the arrow slipped from my fingertips but rolled with laughter moments later as I watched it plow into the ground twenty-five feet in front of the hay bale or else sail high or wide. We never once hit the target or even the bale upon which it was posted. But that was almost beside the point. What mattered was that we were outdoors laughing and carrying on, and that Laura could send a postcard home saying she'd spent the afternoon on the archery range.

That summer, through Roy and Laura and so many others, I got a close-up look at real life and true character. I led wheelchair nature hikes, helped clean out colostomy bags, changed bandages, gave sponge baths, and spoon-fed kids with cerebral palsy who shook so badly that they wore most of their food on their face by the end of the meal. I read bedtime stories to nine-year-old Juan, who ate with a fork between his toes because both arms had been amputated, and sang to little blind Eddie, who had to be watched like a hawk because he often wandered off and climbed trees. I was in awe of each of them, and in their own way they taught me the real meaning of the word *courage*.

Wherever I went, those kids tagged along in my shadow. When they wanted help or company, they asked for me. It wasn't enough that I stood on the beach and supervised their activities. They wanted me in the water with them or to pedal at their side in a pontoon boat. On overnighters, they raced to unroll their sleeping bags beside mine.

They knew I understood their special needs and pains. They knew I understood their desires to stretch their boundaries. They knew I understood, because I was handicapped too. And just as I did my best to help them, so they reciprocated in ways that brought tears to my eyes. Never did I feel more wanted than in the dim light of an evening campfire, when they passed a flashlight from wheelchair to wheelchair, holding it beneath their faces just so I could read their lips and share in their conversation.

At the campfires, they didn't talk about their handicaps but about their friendships and how they hoped to return to camp the following year—all the while knowing that some of them wouldn't live to see another summer.

I marveled at how well they accepted their individual handicaps, carrying their burdens and living content, grace-filled lives. Perhaps their smiles dissipated back in their homes and hospitals amidst the routine of daily life. Perhaps I only saw them during their moment in the sun, those two weeks of camp for which they had waited all year. Nevertheless, I saw their faces absolutely shine. And as I watched their lips move in the amber glow of the flashlight beam, I felt I was in the company of angels.

12

SHADOW OF THE CROSS

The next fall I transferred to Springfield College, a small liberal arts college in Massachusetts that had been founded as a training school for the YMCA. With its small enrollment of under three thousand students, it had a family feel, and everybody seemed to know everybody. Unlike my trial acceptance to Ohio State, I was accepted at Springfield on the basis of my academic record, with no strings attached. I had proven myself. I was college material.

Bordering one side of the campus was a graffiti scarred neighborhood whose homes, insured by Smith & Wesson, all had peeling paint and barred windows. It was an area where you didn't walk your dog after dusk if you cared about your dog, and where people mysteriously disappeared at night, but nobody dared to investigate. On the other side of campus were Norman Rockwell homes with manicured lawns and shade trees—a neighborhood where mothers walked their babies in strollers, cars were washed on Saturdays, and trash was picked up every Wednesday.

My roommate at Springfield was a pudgy New York Pole named Amy who was nearly deaf, though with the help of two hearing aids she could use the telephone if the other party screamed. She had long, shoulder-length black hair, charcoal eyes, and hawkish eyebrows that looked malevolently evil when she cocked them in anger, which was often enough because we drove each other crazy.

Our prime conflict was our study schedule. As a newly declared political science major, I had to wade through stacks of books each semester and often put in all-night sessions. Amy, on the other hand, majored in therapeutic occupation through art, which was a fancy name for rug weaving and macrame design. I never saw her crack a book, but she huffed and fussed about her "rough schedule" and had a stage-ten fit if I didn't turn out the lights each night by eleven o'clock, which I seldom did.

Unlike me, Amy maintained a safe distance from alcohol and pizza. To appease her, I didn't stock any beer in the mini refrigerator we kept in the room, and let her fill it instead with yogurt and bagels.

Though she declined my invitations to various parties, she did agree to go with me one Saturday to the state fair. On our wanderings through the midway, we stopped by a fortune-teller's booth. Amy elbowed me to leave when the man walked over to us, but I was intrigued by his multicolored robe, tattoos, what appeared to be a glass eye, and the red silk scarf knotted snugly around his head.

He glanced first at me, then gazed at Amy with his good eye. "What sign are you, darling?" he asked her.

Amy froze beside me and kicked my leg. She wanted to go.

"What sign are you?" he asked again.

She looked at me nervously, and I could see she was puzzled by the question. Her finger went to her mouth and she bit a nail.

"Well, what are you?"

"I'm Polish!" she blurted, and then glanced at her feet. I could not contain my laughter. It was the best Polish joke I'd ever heard.

One of the only things Amy and I never disagreed about was music. There was nothing we loved more than cranking up the stereo full blast and bathing in the vibrations of Simon and Garfunkel. One night after a flurry of exams, a friend led us word-for-word through the lyric sheet of "Bridge Over Troubled Water" as the record played. We wore her out after a couple of dozen rounds, and when she left the fun started.

I locked the door and turned the stereo volume up as high as it would go. Then Amy and I sprawled out on the floor, holding our hands to the speakers to maximize vibrations. Each time the song ended, I promptly moved the needle back to the start of the song. We howled out the song again and again and again, and turned off the stereo only when we noticed the light of dawn seeping through the window. Then we crawled into bed and slept until midafternoon.

When we finally unlocked the door and stepped outside, we were nearly mugged. It had never crossed our minds that we had put the entire dorm through a night of misery.

"What were you trying to do, blow the windows out?" fellow dormers complained. "We banged and banged on your door."

When we heard that, Amy and I both bit our tongues to keep from laughing. Only hearing people would try to get deaf people's attention by banging on a door!

Three blocks from campus on the broken side of town was a large, beautiful cathedral, whose towering spire cast a shadow of the cross down the street in the late afternoon. Like the yellow brick road leading to Oz, the shadow of the cross formed a path that led straight into the cathedral's cavernous interior, where the sun filtered through the stained glass windows, forming puddles of rainbow light.

One afternoon a week, I met with Father McNamara at the church to learn more about Catholic beliefs and customs. I had hundreds of questions: about kneeling and Communion and confession and Mother Mary and the Trinity. White-haired and patriarchal, he worked with me patiently, even when I explained I couldn't accept certain Catholic teachings that ran counter to my Protestant upbringing.

"The foundation of this church is Jesus Christ," he softly replied. "That is the cornerstone upon which this church was built; other matters are less essential."

After I got to know Father McNamara better, I asked if it would be possible to play the church's pipe organ during the week when it was not in use. Without a second thought, he reached into his desk and handed me a key to the side door. "The organ is yours," he said with a smile.

Several times a week, I let myself into the church during the early morning and late afternoon hours, and I played to my heart's content. The keyboard was as massive as the deck of an aircraft carrier, and the pipes loomed above me like chimney stacks.

I only wish I could have heard what it sounded like, but for me it was enough to feel the vibrations pounding against me like the waves of an ocean, rising through the black and white ivories into my fingers, coursing up my spine, and settling deep inside my brain until my feet got tapping and I started singing at the top of my lungs. I like to think my singing and playing sounded like heaven, but perhaps it was music only to God's ears. To others it may have sounded like trash cans being kicked down a long flight of steps—whatever that sounds like!

Having reached a mutual understanding with Father McNamara about the essentials and nonessentials of faith, I asked to be baptized into the church, which he did one golden autumn Thursday afternoon. As I stood beside the baptismal font and received the mark of the cross on my forehead, I suddenly began to cry and then to sob as painful scenes from childhood flashed through my mind.

I was flooded with memories of being stranded while playing hide 'n' seek; of feeling isolated at the family dinner table amidst laughter or anger; of being made fun of in elementary school by Raymond and Jimmy; of being molested by a depraved family friend; of slipping into homosexuality to maintain friendship; of trying to understand my mother's dark depression; of drinking myself into a stupor to be accepted; of trying so desperately hard to fit into the mold of the hearing, hurting world.

As the memories swept through my mind, I was overcome by my own humanity and longed desperately for the opportunity to lay my burdens down once and for all, to start over again, to have my aches and memories and hurts erased. I wanted to be free not to blame and hate and bear grudges and plot revenge. I ached to be forgiven as much as to forgive others and thereby turn the other cheek.

With tears streaming down my face, I turned to Father McNamara and asked if I could be left alone in the stillness of the cathedral. He placed an understanding hand on my shoulder as I slipped quietly into the front pew by myself, dropped onto my knees, and turned my eyes to the cross.

When I left the cathedral two hours later, my tears had dried, and I felt a tremendous freedom, a sense of purpose, a sensation so breathtaking that for a moment I thought I might possibly be able to fly. At the same time, I was afraid of Mom's reaction. That thought kept my feet firmly planted on the ground.

As days turned to weeks and weeks to months, I felt an inner urging to seek a more contemplative, meaningful life. I still occasionally drank and smoked marijuana, but it satisfied me less and less. It seemed empty and without purpose, almost a cover-up to keep me from thinking about my new-found spiritual sensitivity. Deep inside I felt a tug-of-war being waged, as if opposing forces each had a strong grip on my heart of hearts and the referee yelled, "Pull!"

I lay awake at night, staring down the ceiling and pondering my inner urge to seek a reverential life of prayer and peace. I wanted to flee from the turmoil of peer pressure and the heartache of memories, to discover the true meaning and purpose of life. I knew there had to be a reason why I existed, and that reason had to extend beyond my shallow, fleeting, empty desires.

I found a deep sense of peace and solitude when I was in church. Wherever there was a chapel, I felt I was at home. It was a comfortable, relaxed feeling, as if I'd just entered my front door, hung up my coat, and prepared to sit down at the dining table for a large meal. These feelings were not dependent on the denomination of the church. It just so happened that the closest and most accessible church was Catholic, and when I stepped inside its sanctuary, I felt a pervading sense of calmness, a knowledge that all was well with my soul.

I finally reached the point where I didn't want to let those feelings go. I didn't want to contain my inner joy to Sunday mornings or brief interludes during the week. I wanted to feel it every moment of every day. And so I began to seek a more intimate relationship with God, praying that I could lay aside all personal considerations to discover his will and purpose for my life. In my innermost being, I felt I could do that best in a convent. There I would be free of the entanglements of life and could draw closer to God than anywhere else on earth.

Such a thought was at once so intimate and outrageous that I discussed it with nobody. I knew better than anyone else that I was far from the ideal candidate for the convent. Nobody else was counting, but I knew my list of sins was a mile long. I willingly surrendered to temptation like a weak-kneed child, doing the very things I most despised but feeling powerless to stop.

Nevertheless, I prayed all the harder and quietly began to inquire about various convents in the region.

Several weeks later, on a clear and cool moonless evening, Amy and I set out on a long drive to a Trappist convent in Wrentham, Massachusetts. Looking heavenward at the vast spray of stars as I drove along the straight empty roads, I felt I was on the way to Bethlehem. Amy, on the other hand, thought I was on the road to the biggest mistake of my life. She clicked on the light inside the car so I could read her lips and urged me to reconsider.

"This is a really, really, really stupid idea," her lips said.

"Stupid? Why is it stupid?" I screamed back, steering with my knee.

"You are a college student. You are smart. You have a brain."

"So what?"

"At convents, people don't think."

"At convents, people *pray.*"

"Sue!"

"Amy!"

"Sue! Convents are as dead as . . . as dinosaurs."

I smiled and snapped off the light. I was undeterred and felt at peace within my heart. From deep inside, familiar music rose to my lips, and I began to sing my personal anthem. It was, indeed, a silent, holy night, lit with the jewel light from billions of stars as glories streamed from heaven afar.

The following day we arrived at Mount St. Mary's Abbey, a small, unassuming brick quadrangle that crowned one of the low granite hills some forty miles from Boston. I got out of the car slowly and looked around. The surrounding fields, already plowed under, stretched from horizon to horizon like a dark, moody sea. Rising like buoys out of water, giant oaks stretched toward the sun-drenched sky, their brittle leaves aflame with the reds and oranges of fall. I mouthed a silent prayer and then took a long, deep breath. The air was filled with the smell of the fertile earth and livestock and hay, and from somewhere inside came the warm, familiar scent of baking bread.

I motioned Amy toward the front door, which opened into a small, windowless room. A straight-backed wooden chair sat against one wall between two framed pictures of Jesus, one at the Last Supper, the other of him extending his nail-pierced hands. The other walls were bare. At the front of the room was a simple display case containing handmade greeting cards and a collection of unadorned pottery vases, bowls, and pitchers. Beside them was a sign explaining that donations for the goods should be placed in a small basket atop a nearby ledge and would be used to help sustain the convent ministry. On the wall beside the ledge was a doorbell labeled For Assistance.

Since the grounds were deserted, I rang the bell and waited. When nobody came after several minutes, I rang it several more times. Still there was no response. Amy nudged me and signed, "Dead . . . dead . . . dead." Then she stepped to my side and pushed the doorbell without letting up.

Suddenly, a wooden board above the ledge slid open, and the jowly face of a middle-aged nun turned to glare at us. My heart jumped, but I forced a smile.

193

"Please, please stop ringing that bell!" she demanded. Her lips were tight and without color, and her face remained hard. Amy took her thumb off the bell. "For five minutes I've been asking what you want. Did you not hear me?"

"But you just now opened the—"

"I was speaking, even shouting through the voice box."

I glanced over at the grate in the wooden siding. It suddenly struck me that she'd been there all along, but out of sight.

"I'm very, very sorry," I blurted. "My friend and I cannot hear. We're both deaf."

The woman glanced from me to Amy and then back to me. "You seem to be hearing me fine now."

"No, no, I'm reading your lips."

"Well, I don't . . . ," the woman began, fingering the black rosary beads hanging from her waist as her face flushed. "I don't quite know what to say. I'm all at once quite embarrassed . . . and apologetic if—"

"No, I understand. It's really no problem. I should have explained I was deaf when I called ahead."

"So you're Sue Thomas?" she said, much kinder now as the lines and hard edges of her face softened.

I nodded.

"Sister Mary Eleanor," she said, extending a veiny hand.

After I introduced Amy, the woman ushered me through a side door, which was bolted from the inside. Amy stayed behind, saying she'd walk the grounds or read in the car. We entered a small room, where for the next several hours I sat in a metal folding chair and told the novice teacher my life story: of losing my hearing at about two; the long, tortured process of learning to speak; my brother's sudden disappearance from home; what it was like to be taunted and made fun of in school; my love-hate relationship with my mother; finding solace in the Catholic chapel near the college campus; my baptism; and, finally, feeling the deep inner urge to live within a convent.

The white-and-black robed nun listened patiently. When I finished, she looked me straight in the eye. "My dear child, it is clear to me that you are seeking God, and now we will join you in searching for his desire for your life. There needs to be much prayer. I want to talk with the head superior and have the other sisters pray. Then we will need to correspond back and forth and see what God is leading you to do."

"My heart's desire is for God's will to be done," I said, confident that I already knew God was leading me right to that very spot, and that I would find comfort and serenity among the fifty other nuns who had taken vows of poverty and silence, forsaking everything for a higher calling.

After I departed, we exchanged regular letters for several weeks. In each I reaffirmed my desire to enter the cloistered convent, while Sister Mary Eleanor assured me they were praying. And then one day I got the shock of my life.

"Dear Sue," her next letter began. "You have experienced and suffered much in your young life, and you surely are an inspiration to many, many people. However, after much prayer and the seeking of divine guidance, we feel that our convent is not the best home for you."

"What!" I shouted aloud. I couldn't believe the words I was reading, but there they were in black and white.

"There is another order in Massachusetts that consists of sisters who are handicapped. We feel you would be more at home there, with others who are disabled and have experienced physical struggles similar to your own."

My mind reeled. How could this be! I felt so absolutely certain about my direction, but now a cold letter was telling me that God had other plans for my life. My heart screamed as I tried to fight back burning tears. I'd been rejected because I was deaf. But what was there to hear in a silent convent?

The next several weeks were confused and depressing. My prayers ricocheted within my head like billiard balls, and I felt I was the punch line of some celestial joke. The more I thought about the situation, the more tempted I was to drown my sorrows at the corner bar. But I knew that would merely be a temporary fix and that I'd wake up the next morning with locomotives in my head. I'd been down that path before and knew it was a dead-end solution.

Despite my disappointment, I still wanted to draw closer to God. And if that was not possible with the Trappists, I knew there was another convent out there for me.

13

FORK IN THE ROAD

everal months later I received an invitation to spend a weekend with the Carmelite order in New Hampshire. But I was disappointed as soon as I arrived. Unlike the Trappist convent with its country roots, out-of-doors life-style, and communal farm work, the Carmelites maintained a convent just down the road from a ma-and-pa diner, where the daily $4.95 special was served atop plastic checkerboard tablecloths; a barbershop where blue-jeaned patrons hung their caps on the antlers of a seven-point deer; and look-alike, aluminum sided homes where runny-nosed children still rode tricycles rather than Big Wheels.

The convent, with its boxy brick buildings and sun-blistered carport for visitors, was as plain as the small town that surrounded it. Pulling up the driveway, I spotted a rusted hoe resting alongside a small garden and felt pangs of regret as memories of the vast, plowed acreage surrounding the Trappist convent rolled through my mind. The shrubs and flowers lining the small chapel to the right were too evenly planted to look friendly, and not even the budding leaves waving hello from a scattering of oaks and maples helped overcome my desire to shift into reverse and make a hasty departure.

I sat in the parked car, staring blankly outside for several long minutes. And then with a deep breath, I reluctantly got out, walked through the front door of the convent, and rang the doorbell inside the small and deserted front room. A wooden panel immediately slid open, and a beaming nun led me into a reception area where we were joined by Sister Mary, the head superior.

As I launched into my life story, I fingered the black leather armrest, thinking that I would again be rejected because of my deafness. But my uneasiness was assuaged by Sister Mary's warm, understanding smile, which was reflected on the glowing faces of the other nuns I met throughout the weekend.

"We are living in changing times," she told me later that day when I was ushered through two locked doors into the inner cloister. "And we are trying to change with them," she added. Her lips moved slowly, and I had no trouble reading her every unhurried word. "Even the older sisters have switched to knee-length habits, and the younger ones, well . . . courtesy of Vatican II, they have started making their own clothes. We even have one, a particularly spirited little sister, who sometimes wears a spot of makeup, though I hope it's not contagious."

My eyes followed hers about the private chapel where a half-dozen women in skirts and blouses prayed on their knees. On the slim leg of one—perhaps the spirited one—a gold ankle bracelet glimmered in the candlelight above her white leather sandals.

Because the cloistered life was so entirely different than the secular world, Sister Mary did not want me to

make a sudden, overwhelming life change but to gradually become accustomed to the convent. And so for a
year and a half, I juggled my class schedule so I could
enter the convent as an apostolate for short periods—
sometimes a weekend, other times for a week or two—
as I waited and made sure this was God's direction for
my life. With each visit, I became more familiar with every aspect of the sisters' lives, eating their vegetarian
diet, praying silently beside them, reading Scripture,
singing, sharing in Gregorian chants, and working with
them as they sewed vestments for area priests, baked
bread, made lithographic prints, and carved crucifixes
from downed branches on the property.

Between classes and the convent, I searched for and
then recovered from various exploratory ear surgeries
and new treatments for deafness. Perhaps these proce-
dures worked for some people, but after a while I felt I
was chasing the wind. Nevertheless, I was not disheartened. It was enough for me to hear the voice of God.

At the end of one stay at the convent, Sister Mary
summoned me into her office. "We are praying with
you," she assured me. "Life within this convent is separate and apart from the world you know, and we don't
want you to make your decision in haste."

"This is where I want to make my home," I announced.

She nodded, suddenly becoming more serious than
I'd ever before seen her. "Have you discussed this with
your parents?"

"The final decision is mine," I replied.

"Yes, but they have much at stake in your life and
should not remain uninformed."

"I have spoken with them. I know what they'll say, especially my mother. They won't like it."

"Perhaps not. But their counsel needs to at least be sought, if only for one final time. The reality is that in their eyes you will always be their little Susie. Time doesn't change that, even when you are independent. After informing them of your intentions, if it's your desire to return to us and lead a cloistered life, you will be welcomed. But you must feel no pressure from us to make such a decision. As with you, we desire only what God wants for your life."

"Thank you, Sister Mary," I said, backing slowly away. "I understand."

I dutifully made the eighteen-hour drive home, only to have sparks fly with Mom as soon as I crossed the threshold.

"I don't care where you live. I don't care what you do. Just return to your own church. Come back to the church you were raised in," she begged.

"Mom, I go to a Catholic church because when I needed a church it was the only one open. Do you honestly believe God cares whose sign is on the door, whether Baptist, Presbyterian, Methodist, or Catholic?"

"We're talking about more than a church now. You're closing yourself off from the rest of the world, and I don't understand why. Why would you want to waste your life in this type of environment?"

"Waste?"

"Waste!"

"I just happen to believe . . . with all my heart . . . that by praying for the needs of the world, I can help save us all from the wrath of God. I sincerely believe that."

"Then you're sincerely wrong! God is quite capable of—"

"Let me finish! In monasteries and convents all around the world, not a single minute passes when people aren't praying. At every time of day and night, they're on their knees in intercessory prayer."

"Inter*what?*"

"Intercessory prayer. Praying not just for their own needs, but for those of others, for you and Dad and the boys, for our country and its leaders, for—"

"It's not that we mind you praying, Sue. But why do you need to do it in a convent?"

"I feel at peace there. And in the stillness, I hear God."

"You keep talking about hearing God, but you refuse to hear *me.* I gave up my whole life for you, and now you run off and do something stupid like hide behind a wall with a bunch of hermits who never got married!"

"I'm not hiding!"

"You are hiding!"

"I'm not!"

"I gave you *everything*—everything a mother can give and more. I look at you now and see years of my life invested—so you could be smart and live on your own in the hearing world and not have to depend on us. But once you're actually on your own and have the opportunity to make a smart decision, you run off like an ostrich and stick your head in the sand!"

"I resent that!"

"Sometimes the truth hurts."

"You just don't understand. You never did and never will."

"I understand plenty. I understand that we made a pledge when you were young that we would do whatever we humanly could to help you become as much a part of the hearing world as possible. I understand that now you're turning your back on all that, only to enter a world of silence. I understand that you're throwing your voice away, and with it goes my life and your life."

"The life I live now is lived for God, Mother. For God!"

"Then by God, get your head out of the sand and start living it!" she blasted, turning and running off to her room, where she stayed for the remainder of my visit.

My father was not as harsh, but he was firm. "Susie, you need to quit the convent," he said.

I shook my head. To quit would mean turning my back on God. That was something I couldn't do, even if it meant disregarding my own parents.

"Your mother cannot handle you being there. You *have* to come out. You just cannot do this to your mother."

"What am I doing?"

"She's not taking it well. Please."

I cut my stay short and headed back to the convent, with a new understanding of what my brother must have experienced so many years earlier. I was mad when I finally arrived—mad at Mom for trying to run my life, for ruling over Dad, for driving my brother from home for twenty years, and for making me feel so guilty about following a divine calling. I was an adult, and if I wanted to live in a convent nobody would stop me. Not even Mom.

But before I could tell Sister Mary that I had decided to take my formal vows, another nun tapped me on the shoulder. I glanced up and saw her signal me to follow her. I thought she was summoning me on behalf of the head superior. Instead, she delivered crushing news.

"I just received a phone call from your father," she said. "He asked that you return home as soon as possible."

"But I've just been there."

"Dear child, there is a family emergency. Your mother apparently tried to take her life, and your father said she's in pretty bad shape."

Reluctantly and tearfully, I again packed my bags. I knew whatever had happened had been another ruse of Mom's—a cry for attention just like all the other times. When I finally arrived home, she was in bed as expected. Dad said she'd cried continually after I left, stopped eating, and finally swallowed a bottle of Valium.

"Please don't do this," he said. "Come out of the convent. I can't take it, and I'm afraid for your mother. We're getting older, and . . . Please, Sue, if you feel you have to do this, could you please just wait until after we're *gone?*" His pleading eyes filled with tears, and he wrapped his arms around me.

When he eventually let go, he asked that I go into their bedroom, tell her I was home, and assure her I loved her.

"I'm not going in there," I insisted. "I'm tired of being manipulated by her, of being forced to say I love her. She's not going to run my life!"

"Please, just talk with her," he asked.

Finally, I relented. I stomped to the door and threw it open. Then I paced over to her bed. When I looked down, I screamed. There she lay, with a sheet draped lightly over her body. Her hands were folded on her chest in a funeral pose, and a plastic bag was draped over her head. Her eyes were closed, and she didn't appear to be breathing. I refused to be fooled any longer. It was a desperate act, and I knew it.

Reaching down, I ripped the bag off her face. "You're a fake, an absolute fake!" I screamed. "And you're not going to do it! You're not going to ruin my life! I'm getting out of here, and I'm not coming back!" And then I turned away and stormed out of the house.

I walked the streets of Boardman for an hour before Dad found me. He edged to the curb beside me and opened the car door, but I shook my head and kept walking. He pulled ahead, got out, and came over to my side.

"I'm not going home," I said, bracing my feet.

"You have to come home."

"I won't go."

"Please, Sue. It's going to be OK."

"It will never be OK. Every time it happens, you say it's going to be OK, but it never is."

"Everything's going to work out. I promise you."

My eyes suddenly flooded with tears, and I fell into his arms. He held me tight for several minutes. Finally I stepped back and nodded. "OK, I'll go home with you, Dad. I love you. But I can't face Mom. I just can't be around her."

"Everything's going to be all right," he assured me again as he guided me to the car.

Upon arriving back home, I planted myself like a cold, immovable statue on the living room couch. A few minutes later, Dad was at my side.

"Your mother is in the bedroom," he said. "She wants to see you."

"Absolutely not. I'm not going in there."

"Go talk to her."

"No, Dad. I have nothing to say."

"Please."

"I'm not going in to see her!" I insisted at the top of my lungs. "If she wants to see me, she's got to come out here. I will never, never go back in that bedroom again! Never!"

A half hour later, Mom walked out in her robe and sat near me in the living room. Neither of us said a word. She just sat there, staring ahead at the wall.

Though we didn't talk, it was a turning point in our relationship. I didn't go running to her. She came to me. I suddenly realized she was no longer the final authority over my life, nor was I her little girl. Little Susie had grown up. I now had a mind and will and future of my own that might or might not include her. I was free!

Nevertheless, I knew the future would be difficult for me because Mom's roots were so deeply imbedded in my life. Her love for me surpassed any I had ever known. She had wrapped me in affection as a child that made me feel totally secure. She had provided me with opportunities that would last a lifetime. Yet her legacy of love was conditional. It came with many strings attached.

Without Mom, I would never have graduated from high school, would never have learned to sing or play an instrument, would never have felt the wonder of words in my mouth. Those words and my ability to speak were her gifts to me. Knowing the sacrifices she and my father made, how much did I owe them in return? Did I need to concede to their demands, even if I thought they were wrong?

After I saw Mom, I realized that if I entered the convent for good, she would quite probably end her life. Deep down, I knew I'd be miserable if that hung over my head. I realized, of course, that I could neither control such an action nor be blamed for it. Yet I was overcome with fear that if she succeeded, I would lose the one person who most helped me get through life. At the same time, I didn't want to give in. How could I deny God? By saying yes to my parents, I felt I was saying no to God. Saying yes to God meant saying no to my parents. There was clearly a fork in the road, and a choice of direction had to be made. I felt I was walking an emotional tightrope, and the rope was not all that tight.

That night I threw myself on my bed and cried until my pillow was soaked. Then, in the black stillness of the early morning hours, I gave in. I decided to forget about the convent and all that I had prayed for during the past couple of years.

By choosing not to return, I felt I had failed a test God had placed before me. I had told him I was willing to forsake everything to follow him, even my own family. But in the end, I turned my back on God. I felt like a traitor, a Judas.

I figured God would turn his attention toward those who were more faithful, those who continued saying yes when the rest of the world said no. Like a seed planted in rocky soil, I flourished for a season. But my roots were shallow, and when the sun beat down I withered. I could never again face God. I'd put my hand to the plow in his service but had turned back. He'd seen my back, he'd heard my no. What further use could I be? I was a gargantuan failure, for I'd failed the Creator of the universe. It was my darkest, bleakest hour. I was alone, alienated, and desperately lonely. Without God, I had no hope.

When I returned to Springfield, I spilled the entire story and my feeling of desperation to a friend. I needed somebody to confide in, if only Sherry, who had often said she thought she was an atheist. She understood my pain in human terms but hadn't a clue about the spiritual struggle I faced. "Did you ever stop to think why God gave you a voice?" she asked.

I looked at her blankly. She was the last person I'd expected a sermon from.

"Maybe God wants you out in the world, instead of living behind some wall in silence. You've got a voice, and maybe you should think about using it."

Her words were aimed like a dart and went straight to my heart. Nevertheless, in my vulnerability and feeling of isolation from God, I experienced the very real urge to once again resume my old life-style. Why try to be good if God no longer cared?

14

WHITE LIGHT OF PROMISE

stayed in Ohio long enough to tell my parents I would leave the convent. Then I headed back to pick up where I left off at Springfield College. Feeling separated from God, I was soon living a nonstop party and spending most of my money on food and liquor. I gained weight rapidly and every month bought a larger pair of jeans.

I went through the motions of attending church but couldn't concentrate. Sunday mornings became little more than a ritual of hoping God would somehow give me a sign that my life still mattered. I hoped for something on par with Moses' burning bush—some clear and unmistakable signal. Sensing nothing but silence, I began arriving after the doors closed, sat in a back pew where I couldn't read the priest's lips if I tried, and then bolted during the final prayer. Finally I just quit going.

With the intense pain of leaving the convent and the resulting alienation from my parents, I was desperate for companionship. I needed a friend—any friend. I eventually met a woman whose husband was a university professor. We began confiding in each other, and one day she told me her marriage was on the rocks. The following week, out of the blue, she showed up on my doorstep.

"I'm leaving my husband and need a place to bunk," she said. "Could I stay with you?"

"Sure," I said, and opened the door to what unsuspectingly became a five-year homosexual affair. When the woman's husband discovered our relationship, he stormed over to the apartment late one night. He banged on the door and screamed for all the world except me to hear, working himself into such a rage that I thought I'd be killed. Only when the police came did I relax.

When I told the woman I was scared and wanted to move, she nodded and said *we* could be out and settled elsewhere within a week. She was seven years older than I and had money to spare. I was broke. So I followed her lead even though it led to a dead-end street.

Unlike me, the woman was brazenly open about her homosexuality. All my life I had tried desperately to fit into society. I knew my life-style was nothing to be proud of, but she wanted everybody to know she was a lesbian, and began frequenting homosexual bars. The first time I went with her, I wanted to turn around and run. Men were paired off with other men on the dance floor and kissing in dark corners. Women were doing the same. I felt an immediate revulsion. But after a few drinks I quit worrying about the rightness or wrongness of the situation and stepped onto the dance floor with my friend.

In 1976, eight years after enrolling at Ohio State, I graduated from Springfield College with a double major in political science and international relations. I framed my diploma and hung it in a prominent place on my wall. It was a major accomplishment, and I was excited to see where it would lead.

To my dismay, it led nowhere. I couldn't even find work. After months of job searching, my friend moved with me back to the outskirts of Youngstown, Ohio, about five miles from my parents' house. I naively thought things would be different for me in my home state.

My friend quickly found work as a recreational therapist, while I continued my fruitless search. I followed up on dozens of help-wanted advertisements in the newspaper, applying for everything from secretarial positions to social work. Nobody wanted my help. The barrier was my deafness—my invisible but very real handicap.

I finally started getting nibbles when I stopped writing on the application that I was deaf. But when it came up in interviews, the eyes of the personnel director immediately glassed over. Finally, I began waiting until I was just about to leave before saying anything.

"Oh, I forgot to tell you something," I'd say. "I'm deaf. I read lips."

By waiting, I demonstrated to the interviewer that I could function in his world and answer any question. Nevertheless, I never made the final cut. The reason was always the same: I couldn't use a regular telephone.

I finally had no choice but to apply for government disability, but my application was turned down because I had a college degree and, according to officials, should be able to get a job. I appealed, explaining that nobody would hire me because I was deaf. I then challenged those at the government office either to give me a job or a disability check. They gave me a check.

Though I won the appeal, my victory was bittersweet. I wanted a job, not a handout. As I pondered my own difficulties in finding work, my heart cried for the millions of other deaf and hearing-impaired people around the world who had doors of opportunity closed in their faces. I longed to help bridge the gap between the deaf and hearing worlds, but where would I start? How could I help those who primarily communicated by sign language if I, having a voice, couldn't even get a job?

My relationship with my roommate alternated between love and hate. Deep inside, I didn't want to live with her. But without her, I knew I'd be thrown back into my own silent world. The internal conflict left me feeling as if I had one foot on a dock, the other in a rowboat. And the tide was on its way out.

I thought I'd eventually work up the courage to move out, but time ran out. One day my friend stunned me with an announcement. She was leaving me for another woman. Blindsided by the rejection, I burst into bitter, agonizing tears.

After loading her belongings into her car, she came back inside one final time. I was sitting on the stairs crying when I felt her hand on my shoulder. I looked up.

"You know, someday you're going to thank me," she said. "You and me, we're different. You don't belong in this kind of relationship. Someday you'll realize I did you a favor." She turned slowly and walked away.

Unbeknown to me, she'd called my parents and brother, Bobby, prior to leaving and suggested they come to be with me. Five minutes after she pulled out of my life, the three of them walked in. They gathered around me on the staircase and tried to encourage me.

"I'm going to be OK," I sniffed, struggling not to show I was broken and crushed. "Yes, everything will be fine. There's no problem."

A couple of days later, I stopped by my parents' house and suddenly started crying again. Mom asked what was wrong, and I hesitated. I knew she wouldn't understand. But I was tired of hiding my past and burying my emotion.

"Why don't you and Dad sit down," I finally said. "There's something I want to tell you." I followed them into the living room, dying a thousand deaths as they found seats and looked up at me anxiously. I swallowed hard and then blurted out the truth.

"Maybe you already know, but . . ."

"Yes?"

"Well, for the past five years I've been living as a homosexual. Ever since I left the convent, I—"

"A *what?*" interrupted Mom, looking as if she'd been shot in the back. She glanced at my father, then looked back to me. Her mouth hung open.

"It's true."

"Oh, dear. No, no, no. Don't say such things, such nonsense," she said as the color drained from her face.

"I have to get my life in order, and I don't know how. It will take some time."

Mom just stared and her lips moved, but she wasn't making words. She rose to her feet and turned to the wall as my father kneaded a loose flap of skin at the corner of his jaw.

Having nothing else to say, I got up and walked outside into the backyard. Tears stung my eyes. I was broken, and my parents were too stunned to help. The November sun was bright on my back. Suddenly I felt a hand on my shoulder. I turned around. It was my father. His eyes were also clouded with tears.

"I don't care what you've done or where you've been," he began. "You are still my daughter, and I love you. I will always love you."

Before I could stop myself, I began sobbing. I'd never been the recipient of words so graciously expressed or of love more freely given. My father stood there, looking at me awkwardly. He opened his arms and I fell into them. He pulled me close and held me without letting go. I buried my face against his chest, crying like a baby as a thousand pounds were lifted from my shoulders.

"You really mean that?" I asked. Without drawing back to read his lips, I felt a breath in my hair and his head nodding above mine.

In that moment I breathed a silent prayer, my first prayer in a very long time, thanking God for giving me the wisest, most loving, very best dad in the entire world.

My father's comfort provided a needed respite from my pain, but the reality of my world soon returned. Still without work, I had no idea how long I could live independently without returning home. Having no friends or money, I couldn't shake the feeling that my whole life was falling apart. At night, I stared out the front window. My life seemed as empty as the grassy expanse of the nearby park.

Looking through the heavy branches of the towering pines and maples, I fixed my eyes on the monastery across the street that was home to the priests from the Youngstown diocese. Tucked into an alcove in the side of the building, I noticed a statue of Christ. His arms were outstretched, as if he were saying to me, "Come unto me, all you that labor and are heavy laden, and I will give you rest."

Several years had passed since I'd felt at rest. After leaving the convent, I'd grown tremendously weary— weary of running from God, heavy laden with the guilt and heartache of seeking comfort from troubled relationships. Even though I'd turned my back on God, perhaps—just perhaps—he had not turned his back on me.

As my eyes focused on the statue, I thought of the Samaritan woman whom Jesus had met at the well—the woman who'd been married five times and was living with a man who wasn't her husband. She deserved fire and brimstone, but instead Jesus offered her the living water of his love and forgiveness. When condemnation was expected, she received grace.

If there was hope for her, maybe there was hope for me. Wiping the tears from my eyes, I pulled on my coat and carried a large candle across the street. I placed it on the base of the statue and struck a match. Touching the flame to the wick, I prayed silently that God would forgive me, love me, and help me again feel the warmth of his outstretched arms.

Returning to my apartment, I watched the dim light of the candle shining in the still, silent night. For an entire week the candle burned. Its tiny flame withstood even the wind, providing a beacon of hope for me through six long days and seven dark nights.

The following week when my December disability check arrived, I had less than three hundred dollars to my name. It wouldn't carry me through the month, and I was worried about how I'd make up the difference. But deep inside I felt God assuring me that if he took care of the birds and flowers in the field, he would surely meet my needs.

At the same time, I felt God urging me to give away everything I had. On the surface, it made no sense. I had next to nothing, and I didn't want to ask my parents for help or move out of my apartment. For days I struggled, telling myself that I merely had an overactive conscience, that the voice deep in my heart wasn't God at all. But the thought didn't go away.

Early one evening I cashed the check and walked across the street to the monastery. It was snowing outside, and the flakes iced the branches of the old, tall trees in the park. The cold air bit my nose, and I tugged the collar of my black peacoat tight around my neck.

As I approached the priestly home, my footprints trailed behind me in the snow as if cast in plaster. The street and sidewalks were still and very tranquil. Pushing open the large front door, I was greeted by Father Malone's smile, which warmed me like the radiant glow off a radiator. I was glad to see him because he genuinely had seemed to care when I had talked with him a couple of weeks earlier about my job needs.

Father Malone offered to take my coat, but I explained that I couldn't stay. And then I pulled a folded wad of twenty dollar bills from my coat pocket and extended my hand.

"This is for you," I said. "I feel God wants me to give it all away and hold nothing back."

Father Malone glanced at the money and shook his head. "But you have no job, no income, no—"

"I really feel I need to do this. I *want* to do this."

"But—"

"Please, it's no longer mine. For me to keep it now would be wrong."

"So be it," he said, placing his hand on the shoulder of my snow-dusted jacket and looking at me with kind and gentle eyes. "Your gift means more to me than you will ever know. I just pray that through the giving, you will be richly blessed."

The moment I placed the money in his hand, I felt tremendous peace—the satisfaction of knowing I had listened to God's inner urging and acted accordingly. As for my own needs, I knew I needn't worry. The one who multiplied a young boy's loaves and fish to feed multitudes some two thousand years ago was certainly capable of providing daily bread for me.

After I got back on my feet emotionally, I finally sought work at the only place in town I thought I could be hired: the Youngstown Hearing and Speech Center where, more than twenty years earlier, I had learned to speak as a child. When I entered the building, I peered inside the therapy rooms off the main hallway. I saw the little chairs in front of the big mirrors and thought of my own painful sessions with Miss Vetterle. I remembered her piercing eyes, no-nonsense attitude, and how her steel-gray hair shook when I didn't say a word right.

Now there were other children in the chairs, other therapists at their sides, other parents in the hall. An odd, sinking feeling swept over me as if I'd stopped by my old house only to be greeted by a dark-haired woman who didn't look a thing like Mom, to see strange kids climbing in *my* crab apple tree, and to wonder how anybody could paint *my* porch green.

When I knocked on the office door, it was opened by a man I didn't recognize. After introducing myself and telling him of my background and current job need, he said everybody I'd known at the center was long gone and that he was the new director. With that, I thought my chance of being hired went up in smoke. But in the next breath, he told me he needed a part-time counselor in the social services department—somebody to help parents work through the emotions of having a deaf child. His only concern was my inability to use a standard phone. I'd heard that line so often that it was no longer a threat.

"Nothing to worry about," I said. "If the call is critical, others can cover for me. I'm willing to give it a try if you are."

He looked at me skeptically for a long moment and then broke into a wide smile. "You're hired!"

I started the next Monday, and the work I did was far more than just a job. It was an opportunity to give back something of what I'd received from the center. As I met with parents and shared their tears, I understood the heartache my parents had felt so many years earlier. I shared with these young couples my own experience at the center and my thankfulness for those years despite the anguish. To them, my life represented a spark of hope.

"Our child can become just like you," some said. But I knew many families were unable to afford or make the necessary sacrifices for their children to become like me. My goal was not to create little clones of Susan Thomas but to encourage parents to help their children reach their full potential, whether they communicated by signing or speaking.

While working at the center, I was introduced to the parents of deaf children who were deaf themselves. I wanted to help them and become involved in their lives too. But there was a language barrier. They couldn't speak well enough for me to read their lips, and I had never learned sign language—not because I didn't want to, but because my parents had wanted me to speak.

Through an interpreter, I expressed my desire to learn sign language to the Tavalarios, a kindhearted deaf couple in their sixties. Their response was immediate. They volunteered to open the door for me into their world and to teach me to sign.

Two nights a week, the Tavalarios took me to their deaf club, which met in a large room atop the local hangout of the Hell's Angels. It was a perfect arrangement, because who but the deaf could stand the roaring engines? I'd been forewarned that the motorcycle gang had accepted the deaf people and didn't bother them, but I was nervous and scared the night of my first visit.

A fingernail moon hung in the black sky as the three of us parked and walked toward the building. A flurry of moths beat against the lone streetlight on the block. It was the only sign of life between us and the motorcyclists. At the end of the street I saw men in their dark leather, leaning up against the building or drinking beer atop their black bikes. The smell of smoke hung in the air.

I dug my hands deep in my pockets as we approached. The orange tips of their cigarettes lit their bearded faces. Thick heavy chains and sheathed knives hung from their belts. My nose filled with the smell of leather and beer and gas and grease, of smoke and body odor, of distant roads and the wild outdoors. I saw some women out of the corner of my eye. They wore tank tops and black leather, and their hair was long and windblown. Heads turned as we passed, but my eyes were glued straight ahead. I stepped closer to my companions.

Mr. Tavalario gestured with his hand to a flight of stairs. Two Hell's Angels were sitting on the lowest steps, sucking a bottle of beer. They were as big and hairy as a pair of buffalo. Strapped against their thighs were knives longer than any Mom ever had in the kitchen.

Mr. Tavalario headed straight for them. I winced, not knowing whether he would sign for them to please move, step between them, or get us all killed. My heart pounded in my head as I watched. And then an amazing thing happened. As we stepped closer, the two gang members simply stood up and let us pass. To me, it was no less a miracle than the parting of the Red Sea. Mr.

Tavalario nodded his thanks and motioned for me to lead the way up the stairs.

At the top of the long flight of stairs, a dim crack of light shone from beneath the door. I glanced over my shoulder, and Mr. Tavalario nodded for me to enter. My heart started thudding again. Taking a here-goes-nothing breath, I turned the knob. A cloud of smoke poured out. Inside I saw ghostlike images moving through the cigarette fog but could make out no faces.

The Tavalarios guided me inside and took a seat at a card table beside another couple in their seventies. I watched Mr. Tabbie's hands flash and gesture, then the couple looked at me and signed something back. The other man then pulled a deck of cards out of his pockets, shuffled, and the foursome began playing a game I didn't recognize.

Six other tables were scattered throughout the room, and at each sat two aging couples playing what appeared to be the same card game. They played for an hour, then rotated partners. When a new couple took their seats beside the Tabbies, there was the same back and forth flurry of hand motions, the glance in my direction, and the shuffle of cards. With nobody to talk to, I felt isolated and lonely—more lonely than I'd felt in the hearing world.

I suddenly perked up when the man at the table tapped me on the shoulder and made a drinking motion with one hand. *Would I get him something to drink?* I pointed to him and repeated the motion to confirm my thoughts. He shook his head, pointed to me, and made the drinking sign again. *Did I want something to drink?* I pointed to myself, and he smiled and nodded. I smiled and nodded my agreement, and he arose from his chair. When he returned with a Coke and set it beside me, I nodded and smiled again. He nodded and smiled back and then turned his attention back to the cards.

Wanting to demonstrate my thanks without another round of nods and smiles, I reached over and emptied his ashtray into a metal trash can. The man tapped me on the shoulder and pointed to the red plaid ashtray. Then his hands moved. I repeated the motion as best I could, and he corrected me. I did it again, and he nodded and smiled. I thought I had probably just learned the sign for emptying the ashtray, but I wasn't sure.

After my second Coke, the woman at the table flashed her hands at me and stood up. I was puzzled and it showed. She motioned for me to follow and led the way to the bathroom. Inside, I tapped her on the shoulder and made the same hand motions I'd seen at the table. She nodded and smiled and pointed me to a stall. Later, on the way out, she taught me the signs for mirror, hot and cold water, washing hands, and open and closed doors.

Throughout the rest of the night, various couples began teaching me the rudiments of sign language. They pointed at things about the room and signed—a light bulb, a shoe, a woman, a couple—and had me repeat the signs. When I got it right, even when I didn't know what I was signing, they smiled and nodded like eager parents coaxing the first words from an infant.

And so it went, two nights a week for several months, until I was able to converse without using my mouth. Initially, our discussions were very elementary. "How are you tonight?" somebody would ask. "I'm fine. How are you?" I'd respond. If I got stuck on a word, I wrote it on paper or drew a picture, and they showed me the proper sign. Bridging the gap between us was a slow, time-consuming process, like learning a foreign language without texts, but I was thrilled to begin communicating with people who shared many of my same needs, desires, hopes, and heartaches.

Having mastered sign language, I turned my attention to improving my counseling skills and began taking graduate courses at Case Western Reserve in Cleveland, Ohio. But shortly after starting classes, a fellow worker at the center told me about a new FBI program for the deaf in Washington, D.C. She said she'd been contacted by Virginia Lewis, a woman who interpreted for the deaf at presidential and congressional functions. Her new assignment was to train deaf people to classify fingerprints.

My friend asked if I was interested. Though she only had sketchy details about the job, she relayed that I'd be trained by FBI agents and that the pay was great. Listening to her talk was like a dream come true. I was tired of my hand-to-mouth existence. And with a degree in political science and international relations, I'd always harbored a desire to someday work in government. But that desire always seemed about as practical as wanting to be five-foot-ten, with Cover Girl looks and the world's most even tan.

Knowing the per capita income for the deaf was below poverty level, I had long ago lowered my expectations to match that reality. Maybe dreams came true for hearing people, I figured, but not for the deaf. That reasoning changed when I was asked to apply for the job in Washington.

I was suddenly faced with a choice: to remain at the center and earn my master's degree in counseling or to set out for the nation's capital. Though I had tremendous emotional ties to the center, I knew I couldn't stay. I filed a formal application with the FBI, which included reams of paperwork, exhaustive interviews, and a personal background check that began with my immediate family and then expanded like a nuclear chain reaction to teachers, friends, and people I didn't even know I knew.

My worst fear was that something would be discovered about my rocky past. I felt horrible, thinking that terrible mistakes I'd made would haunt me the rest of my life. Could I never start over? I knew the answer to that question and resigned myself to staying in Youngstown. But three weeks later I was notified that I'd been cleared by the FBI! Years of rejection were behind me. Shining before me was the white light of promise.

15

PENNSYLVANIA AVENUE

After tearful farewells with my family, I pulled away from my sleepy hometown in a new 1980 van my parents helped me buy. In the back were all of my possessions, along with four dogs I had acquired over the past five years. I was extremely close to my dogs, especially Prince, a show-quality Irish Setter I'd received as a college graduation present. We understood each other without language. He accepted me for who I was, made no demands, and always greeted me with a wagging tail.

Prince sat beside me in the front seat as we headed out of town. I watched Boardman drop away behind me in the rearview mirror, and with it a lifetime of memories. I didn't know what lay ahead, other than the immediate eight-hour drive, but I was filled with excitement and abounding optimism as I pulled onto the freeway and followed the signs toward Washington.

Realizing that no apartment in the Washington vicinity would accept my dogs, I settled in the Virginia countryside, renting a carriage house on a tree-studded, six-hundred-acre plantation. My first day of work, I was so captivated by the majesty and sweeping panorama around me that the two-hour commute seemed like a trip to the grocery store.

Heading past the White House as the early morning sun glinted off the Capitol rotunda behind me, I felt overwhelmed with awe. Everywhere I looked were buildings and monuments I'd previously seen only in dusty textbooks and on television. One moment I was passing the Washington Monument and Supreme Court; the next, the Smithsonian Institution and Library of Congress. I felt connected, a part of history. For the first time in my life, my pulse raced with excitement as I contemplated the future.

Upon arriving at the J. Edgar Hoover headquarters building on Pennsylvania Avenue, I spent the first hours of my bright new future being fingerprinted, photographed, tagged for security, and sequestered with stacks of personnel forms. After a red-carpet tour and lunch, I was finally ushered into a classroom to begin training with eight other deaf people, all signers, who were part of the new program.

The pomp and intrigue ended as soon as I discovered exactly what we were supposed to do. Projected on a huge screen was a blown-up image of a fingerprint. Its loops and ridges loomed before us like a giant maze as the instructor explained the various patterns.

"What you see here is a central pocket loop, one of eight basic fingerprint patterns," she said, as the interpreter signed beside her for the other trainees. "Once that pattern is identified, you then count the lines from delta, the outside ridge, to the core. This print, then, is a central pocket loop with a count of thirteen," she continued. "This classification, together with the ridge detail, is what makes this print unique. Like a snowflake, it is one of a kind!"

She explained that more than twenty-two thousand sets of fingerprints were received daily by the FBI, and that our job was to make the preliminary classification. We would examine each individual finger impression, code the specific pattern, and then route the print for filing.

I looked down and studied my own right index fingertip. It was a loop with a count of twenty-one. I yawned. My left was a plain whorl with a count of seventeen. My interest in the unique nature of fingerprints dissipated long before my lunch had digested. Devoting my life to sorting loops from whorls seemed as stimulating as sorting apples from oranges. Having seen one fingerprint, I figured I'd seen them all.

I also figured out why the deaf were selected for such a "brain intensive, high security" program. Somebody probably concluded during a late-night brainstorm that we'd do a superb job because we would not be distracted by ringing telephones, closing doors, shuffling papers—or, for that matter, yawns of disinterest or the screams of those driven insane by the task.

I phoned my parents to tell them of my frustrations, but they encouraged me to stick it out. In actuality, they enjoyed telling their friends I worked in a *classified* job for the *FBI* in *Washington, D.C.* It sounded impressive and provided no hint of my eight-to-five drudgery.

I feigned interest for as long as I could, but after sorting several hundred prints, I confided to my supervisor that it didn't take a Sue Thomas to do my job. I politely explained that I had not struggled through voice therapy and college, nor left the convent and quit a job at the Youngstown Hearing and Speech Center only to spend my life counting ridges between the delta line and core. She nodded, scribbled something on a notepad, and smiled thinly at me. I assumed that was her way of telling me to return to work and await my pink slip.

A few days later, I was reassigned to the FBI's typing pool. My job was to enter data into the computer, which was only marginally more interesting than what I had been doing. A couple of weeks later, I again said something to my supervisor. This time the response was more direct.

"This is your second job change in as many months," she said. "If you can't or rather *won't* work here, you'll have to leave the FBI."

I nodded in acknowledgment.

The following day I was not surprised when she tapped me on the shoulder and told me I was wanted at the front office. My mind flashed back to elementary school when I was sent to the principal's office, only to be punished for something that wasn't my fault. I knew without asking that I'd just entered my last bit of data into the computer.

On my way down the long corridor, I wondered whether I should have just kept quiet. Saying I wasn't challenged was certainly honest, but at least it was a job. Perhaps my parents were right. Maybe I should have stuck it out. But as I entered the office, I knew such sentiments came too late.

A secretary guided me through a side door. I was suddenly face to face with seven men, including the head agents for the two divisions I'd worked for. All of them wore dark suits and were sitting around a long table. This was worse, far worse than the principal's office. This was a firing squad! I steeled myself to keep from crying as I stepped into the room.

To my surprise, the men all stood up and offered me a chair. I could tell by their suits and security tags that they were all agents. Maybe I was in bigger trouble than I thought. But why would they stand up? I was suddenly very confused.

They began with small talk, asking me how I had adjusted to the move, how I liked Washington, and whether I was happy working for the FBI. I explained that I wasn't particularly challenged with either the fingerprinting or data entry jobs. As the preliminaries continued, one of the agents expressed his amazement at my lipreading ability.

"Do you ever watch television?" another asked.

"If I'm not too tired by the time I get home," I replied.

"So you can follow what's on the screen?"

"I have problems with accents, but if the lips are visible, I can generally read them."

"Do you go to movies?"

"Sometimes on weekends."

"How does that compare with watching television?"

"I do better, because the lips are much, much bigger," I said, drawing smiles around the table.

One of the men who hadn't spoken looked at me. "You're probably wondering what you're doing here and why we're asking you these questions."

"That did cross my mind."

"Well, we have a situation that you may be able to help us with," he began. "It concerns a video. We filmed a transaction between one of our agents and two suspects in a current case, but the camera's sound mechanism failed. All we have is footage of three people talking, but we can't understand what was said. So we were wondering if . . ."

"If I could watch the video and tell you what's going on?"

"Exactly."

"I'd be happy to help. If there is anything I could use to enlarge the picture, that would be appreciated."

"Equipment is no problem," the man said. "And if you're willing, we'd like you to begin work this afternoon."

After lunch, I was sequestered in a side room off the head agent's office, where a projector and screen were already set up. An assistant demonstrated how it worked, and there sure *wasn't* any problem with the equipment. The image could be shrunk to nearly a bare spot, run at variable speeds, or enlarged to fill a 100-foot screen. Special state-of-the-art magnifying equipment was also provided that prevented the loss of detail when the picture was blown up.

Several times a day, the head agent asked me if there was anything I needed, with emphasis on the word *anything*. I asked for and received three-day weekends. I shifted to evening hours so I could miss the heavy traffic. A driver was even assigned to take me out for dinner, or I could have it catered in—all at the FBI's expense.

The case on the video dealt with illegal gambling operations in Las Vegas. Organized crime was involved, and a lot of money was offered as a bribe. At one point,

the bad guys opened a large briefcase. Inside were untold thousands of dollars, all in neatly banded stacks of
twenty-dollar bills. Everything was pure Hollywood,
and I simply jotted down the dialogue word by word.

After completing that project, I began working with
the FBI's surveillance program. Using specially
equipped vans, agents shot videos of various suspects
talking in the park, driving, and even walking down the
street. Again, I simply watched the tapes and tran-
scribed what they said.

As word about me spread, I was asked to review videos in the Virginia office. One day a large black car
pulled up to the J. Edgar Hoover building, and I slipped
into the backseat with two special agents. At the other
end, the driver whipped through a secret mazelike en-
trance to the garage, and I was whisked through security like a member of royalty. After being debriefed, I
watched a couple of silent clips, narrating the dialogue
as it went. When we were done, the roomful of agents
looked at me as if I possessed some very large and important talent. Little did they know I was just a young
woman from Ohio who learned everything I knew because of my parents and a driven old woman named
Miss Vetterle.

The following week I was called into the head agent's
office in Washington and asked to help with an extremely sensitive project. When I consented, he explained he had obtained footage of two high-level
government officials who were suspected of various
drug and espionage violations.

"You mean, spies?" I asked.

"Well, I . . . ," he demurred.

"I've always wanted to know what a real spy looks like," I said.

The video was much more difficult to transcribe than anything I'd previously seen. One of the suspects had a bushy mustache that obscured most of his upper lip. The other kept his head down much of the time. Some of the conversation was inside a darkened room; at other times, outside in the harsh light of the noon sun. Seldom were they standing still. They were pouring drinks, watching television, walking on the beach, answering the phone. Almost every angle was bad, as if the cameraman purposefully tried to make my job harder.

Day by day I made it a bit farther through the tape. I captured a passing comment about a dog here, a name of a store there. Hardly any sentence was complete, and when I pieced the phrases together, nothing seemed to flow. I went back over it dozens of times, using the magnifiers and enlarging the suspect's lips until they filled the huge screen. It was like piecing together a jigsaw puzzle.

Though I was able to capture about 80 percent of what I could actually see, the conversations still seemed disjointed. Something seemed wrong, but I kept telling myself that lips don't lie. I reluctantly turned my notes into the head agent and explained my misgivings. He didn't seem too concerned and said he would have a secretary type my notes, and that I was to report to his office the following morning at ten o'clock.

When I arrived, I felt nervous. He was waiting for me in the side room and asked me to sit at the table. He took the seat beside me and pulled my typed notes from his briefcase.

"I've reviewed everything you've done on this case, Miss Thomas," he began. "It was a difficult assignment, but you passed with flying colors."

"I *passed?* Passed what?"

He opened another folder. Inside was a sheaf of papers similar to my notes, except the disjointed phrases had been filled in. All the sentences were complete.

"This is a word-for-word transcript of what the two men actually said. I've compared it with your work, and found you were amazingly accurate. Virtually every word was on target. And I've got to say—"

"Wait, wait, please. I don't understand. You say you've got an exact transcript of the video, but how?"

He smiled. "We made this whole thing up as a sort of test. The suspects were our own agents. They were role-playing. We had a transcript of everything they said. We just wanted to see if you were actually reading lips."

"So you thought I was making everything up?"

"By no means. But with the FBI, everything isn't always as it seems. Internal surveillance is a necessary evil in this line of work," he said, clapping me on the shoulder. "Don't worry, though. As I said, you passed."

Having proven I was trustworthy, I became involved in higher-profile cases. The special agents were so impressed that we sometimes even hung out together at the airport for fun after work. If we encountered suspicious activity, I wandered closer and read the people's lips. The late nights cemented our friendships and gave us something to hoot about to break the seriousness of our day-to-day work.

Another deaf person was eventually brought in to work with me, but he didn't have the level of lipreading ability to be successful. Before long I was on my own again. However, there were not enough cases to keep me busy full-time, and I was asked what I wanted to do when I wasn't watching tapes or on surveillance missions.

I knew I couldn't go back to the fingerprint or data entry departments. Wanting more public contact, I asked to become a tour guide. My suggestion was greeted with bemused looks, as if I'd made a grab to become the director of the FBI. The agent politely explained that was not possible because of my deafness and then inquired what else I had in mind.

"Nothing, really. My deafness would not interfere."

"But the tours are nearly an hour long. About fifty people go on each one, and everybody asks questions."

"And I would read their lips and answer the questions."

"I'm sorry, but—"

"I can do it. I really can."

"I don't think it's possible."

"We'll never know unless you let me try."

Because of my surveillance work, I knew they didn't want to lose me. I negotiated for all I was worth and was grateful to be supported by the agent in charge of tour functions, Jeff Maynard. Though his bosses didn't back his recommendation, he asked that I be allowed to attend the training sessions. If I passed, a guide job would be waiting. If not, I'd go back to the typing pool. It seemed fair enough, and his superiors consented.

For the next three months, I participated in an intensive training program. It put me back into a classroom situation where, once again, I was lost. Jeff realized I was sinking fast and assigned another tour guide, a young woman named Denise, to assist me. After every classroom period, we had long review sessions. She was a walking encyclopedia, even knowing how many toilets were in the building and the number of bullets used each year by the entire Bureau.

During one session before a major exam, she asked me thirty key questions. If I didn't know the answer, she quickly volunteered it. The following day, I was surprised to find the same questions on the test. When I later asked Denise about it, she looked at me blankly.

"Did you know those questions would be on the test?" I asked again.

"Jeff said I was to get you through the class," she said. "My assignment was to ensure you graduated—no matter what."

Not surprisingly, I graduated near the top of the class and began leading tours the following week. I was sick to my stomach the night before my first tour and sweated like a horse as I stepped before the group of fifty people in my gray skirt and blue blazer. On the pocket was a patch with the FBI motto: "Vitality, integrity, and truth." I was filled with so much vitality that my knees shook like a small tree in a windstorm!

Forcing a smile to cover my nervousness, I launched into a quick historical overview of the Bureau, then explained the tour would conclude in the firing range with a demonstration of the .38 caliber service revolver and a submachine gun. Just before heading out, as everybody was all smiles, I added one additional thing. "Oh, I forgot to tell you something. I'm deaf."

I loved that point. Smiles suddenly faded, jaws dropped, and the crowd went dead. I didn't make a move. And then I casually assured them not to be alarmed. "I'll be able to answer all of your questions, but you must first get my attention. Tap me on the shoulder, raise your hand, jump up and down—whatever it takes. You see, I read lips."

And then I turned to the person standing next to me. "Hey, where are you from?" I asked, loud enough for the rest of the group to hear.

"California."

"Hey, he's from California. Anybody else here from California?"

With that, smiles returned and we were off and running. My only trouble was understanding the accents of foreign tourists. If I couldn't read their lips after two tries, I'd ask a very American-looking person to repeat the question. People appreciated my candor and vulnerability, and I was grateful for their understanding and backup support. They never let me down.

Virtually overnight, I went from being a perspiration-soaked tour guide to an instant success. Feature articles were written about me in FBI magazines and publications, and I became one of their leading public relations spokespersons. Letters praising my performance and commending the FBI for hiring handicapped people in visible posts poured into headquarters. Month after month, I generated more positive letters than anybody else in the department. I was even consulted by Pentagon officials on how they could better meet the needs of the handicapped.

I reveled in the publicity and attention and was invited to many black-tie parties and social events. My life and struggles in Ohio seemed like a long-forgotten dream. Affirmed and respected, I thought life couldn't possibly get any better.

But not everything was as it seemed. . . .

16

HIGH SOCIETY

The woman who owned the Virginia estate on which I lived had been married to a brigadier general in the Marines, but when he died she was left on her own, at seventy, to manage the property. Three years before I arrived, her loneliness was compounded when her daughter was brutally murdered in her Georgetown home.

To blot out her loneliness and painful memories, she drank until she was numb. Having done the same thing myself in years past, I understood her desperation. As I witnessed my own behavior lived out in the flesh and blood of another human being, I realized how truly pathetic I must have appeared to others. One night she pulled into the drive with a car that was a mass of twisted metal. I ran outside to see if she was hurt.

"I had a lill accidennn," she said, clenching a Bloody Mary in her leathered hand as she climbed out of the car. I watched her sadly, longing for her to wake up and realize how dangerous and ugly heavy drinking was. If it didn't kill her, I thought she'd surely kill somebody else if she continued to drink and drive.

It seemed as if everybody I met in the area drank like fish. From the time they woke up, they began stirring pitchers of Bloody Marys. I tried to acquire a taste for them, but the horrible concoction of tomato juice, tabasco sauce, and vodka smelled worse than sewer water. Finally I quit trying to convince myself it was anything other than a polite way to get sauced before breakfast.

Several months after I'd moved in, my landlady confided to me that her daughter was buried on the property, which I dismissed because she was sloshing drunk. But she insisted on showing me the grave. Still skeptical, I followed her around to the side yard of her Great Gatsby home, holding her arm to keep her from tumbling headlong onto the brick pathway. At seventy, her skin was loose and thin and seemed to crackle at my touch like a plastic grocery bag.

Walled with a six-foot hedge, the yard opened at the far end onto what appeared to be a small private garden. A perfume-scented cherry tree grew tall in the corner, its branches cloaked with white blossoms as delicate as frost stars. These fairy-queen flowers were scattered about its base like Hansel and Gretel crumbs catching the morning dew. The woman pointed. I looked. Buried flush in the lawn was a brass marker, engraved with the girl's name and dates.

Not knowing quite what to say, I simply said, "I'm sorry."

"Sorrr ferrr what?" she slurred.

"For your daughter's untimely death, for your loss."

"Oh, hell," she said, a distant look glazing her eyes. She stood for several minutes, staring at nothing in particular. When she returned from her time travels, she said, "I come here everrr day." I nodded but remained

silent. "Everrr day I brinnn fresh flowers." I nodded
again. She mumbled an expletive, and then we turned
and retraced our steps.

Neighboring estates were owned by corporate chief-
tains and congressional leaders, as well as those who'd
amassed fortunes from third and fourth generation
companies. Others had never worked a day in their life,
but still lived in mansions where money flowed like tap
water. That brought problems of its own. I was no more
surprised to hear that neighbor so-and-so was found
hanging from the rafters than I was to learn that a phi-
landering horse trainer was shot through the head by a
jealous husband who caught him sowing wild oats with
his wife.

I saw emptiness everywhere around me. Living
nearby was a young man who lived off a trust fund
worth untold millions of dollars. Perfectly happy to
drink and party his life away, he had no job, no friends,
and barely spoke to his wife.

One evening when my parents were visiting, he
joined us for a game of cards. Several hours later, the
headlights of his wife's car swung into view.

"Connie's here," I announced.

"That's OK, let's keep playing," he said, without looking up.

I tried to keep up with the old money life-style of the
area but quickly discovered the folly of that. The first
steeple chase my landlady invited me to was right out
of a fairy tale. Sitting at the edge of a vast pasture that
had been roped off for the race, I was surrounded by

neighbors in their hunter green plaids and navy blazers. Their Thanksgiving-sized picnics were spread before them on bone china and served by white-gloved butlers. There was more gold around the women's necks than at Ft. Knox, and their diamonds rivaled the Tower of London's crown jewels.

At such gatherings, I met and mingled with the elite of Washington. At first I was impressed. It wasn't long, however, before the events merely seemed like a grown-up version of my elementary school show-and-tell time. I remembered how fellow classmates constantly tried to outdo each other. They brought in their best doll or their biggest, shiniest new toy. In Washington, the toys were just bigger: new Jaguar, diamond brooch, Arabian horse. You'd stand around and *ooh* and *aah,* and then somebody would mention something about a new summer home they'd just bought or slip in a few words about their daughter having just graduated from Harvard.

Slowly but surely, I became involved in their world, but it was increasingly apparent that I didn't belong. One day my landlady invited me to a Fourth of July lawn party. Since my parents were scheduled to visit the same weekend, I asked if it would be possible for them to attend with me.

By her reaction, you'd have thought I'd asked for the deed to her home. In no uncertain terms, she said I advertised my ignorance of etiquette by even *asking* such a question, and that the request was *strictly* denied because the party had been planned for *months*, every detail had been checked and *rechecked,* the guest list was *perfectly* balanced, and just *who* did I think I was anyway?

"However, I would still request that you attend," she added as an aside. "It's important for the guest list."

When my parents arrived, I explained the situation to them. Since I hadn't already declined the invitation, they felt I was obligated to go as planned. And so I did, but only for about three and a half minutes. The moment I stepped onto the lawn and saw my landlady in the distance, I turned around and walked right back. If her party was not good enough for my parents, it was certainly not good enough for me.

This Queen of the List was not above crashing a party herself, however. One night when I was having a casual get-together for friends, my door suddenly swung open. Standing in the doorway was my landlady, dressed to kill in a beautiful fur and bedecked with several pounds of jewelry. She looked as sadly out of place as a donkey at church, and I knew at a glance that she'd been drinking heavily.

My friends flashed looks asking, "What do we do now?" I shrugged and watched as she edged toward the kitchen, all the while running her finger along the wall for balance. Suddenly she teetered, and a hand darted out to grab her. She smiled a crooked smile and then collapsed in a chair. When she realized somebody was already in it, she laughed till I thought she'd have a stroke. Eventually she quieted down and allowed two of my friends to escort her home.

"Thannns verrr mush," she said to me on her way out the door. "Had a wonnerful time. Thanns for a fine, fine parrry."

While at the FBI, I developed some medical problems and eventually had to have a complete hysterectomy.

I was crushed to think I could never have children of my own—no girls to teach to play the piano or sing, no boys to fish or play catch with. There would be no skating lessons, no hide 'n' seek, no sledding down candle-lit hills. Nobody to make kites for or hang tinsel with.

Being assigned to the maternity floor at the hospital added insult to injury. Everywhere I looked, adoring mothers and fathers cuddled their newborns. I couldn't get to my room without first passing the nursery, where rows of bassinets overflowed with young life, reminding me of the void deep in my body and the joy that would never be mine.

I found it hard to care about my job when I eventually returned. I went through the motions of doing what I was paid to do, but my heart wasn't there. Instead of rushing to arrive in the morning, I found myself noticing more of the world around me. In the early morning hours, I saw between six and thirty deer grazing in the dew-covered fields, their milk chocolate fur aglow with dusty rose light of dawn. Had they been there all along? Perhaps, but I'd never bothered to notice.

One morning an eagle swooped down from the skies and glided beside my car at eye level, its talons poised. Like a fighter jet on touch-and-go exercises, it brushed the ground and came up with a huge black snake dangling from its dagger claws. I was so breathless that I stopped the car until the glorious bird and its prey disappeared over a far rise of corn. That morning I was a half-hour late for work.

Meanwhile, my finances were in total disarray—in part because of my medical expenses but mostly because I stupidly tried to keep up with the Joneses. When I received an expensive gift, I reciprocated in kind. I bet with everybody else at the steeple chases but always lost because I picked horses based on beauty, not speed.

As my bills piled up, even my grocery checks started bouncing. I finally wised up and quit writing checks. If I didn't have money for groceries, I didn't eat. When I ran out of wood to heat my cottage, I chopped up my two deck chairs and stuffed them into the wood-burning stove to keep from freezing.

When I was late with my rent, my landlady was initially tolerant because she knew I'd been in the hospital. "Don't worry about anything," she told me one day when she was sober. "You're a nice person, and I enjoy your company. We'll just forget about the whole thing. I know this isn't intentional."

However, her mood changed faster than the weather when she was fueled by alcohol. When I bumped into her two days later, her face clouded over and turned thunderstorm mean. Moments later her rage burst and I was showered with a string of expletives. Then her lips screamed that she would have *nobody* living off her for free and that if I didn't quit trying to get sympathy with some absolutely *lame* hospital story and pay up *now,* she would take legal action so fast it would make my head *spin.*

I told her on the spot I would leave before the month was out. It was the right thing to do. With medical problems compounded by financial problems, I couldn't help but think there was more to life than Washington and the FBI, even if I didn't quite know where to find it. A week later, my landlady apologized for her outburst and tried to talk me into staying. But my mind was made up.

The soap opera life-styles I saw in Washington and Virginia forced me to take a closer look at myself. I longed to quit pretending I was something I wasn't. I wanted to reestablish my weed-eaten spiritual roots and regain control of my time. Due to my health problems, I was keenly aware of my own mortality and didn't want to spend four precious hours of each day commuting to Pennsylvania Avenue. Not even a great job like mine was worth that kind of sacrifice. I simply wanted to be happy and fulfilled and at peace with myself and my God.

I'd been attending a nondenominational Bible church in nearby Sterling, Virginia. I purposefully went there rather than a Catholic church because I wanted to ease the tension with my parents. I missed the familiar liturgies, along with the candles and beautiful stained glass windows. But the Bible church service was filled with a vitality I'd not experienced before. There, faith came alive. One church or denomination wasn't better than the other. They were just *different.*

As I discussed my feelings and circumstances with the pastor of the church, he suggested that I take a break from work for a year or two and attend classes at the Columbia Bible College seminary in South Carolina. He said seminary wouldn't force me to become a missionary to Zimbabwe or anything like that but would help me develop deep roots to keep my life stable no matter what the future brought.

I investigated further and decided that's what I wanted to do. I remembered the time when, as a child, I had vowed someday to build God a church. Perhaps seminary was the first step in that process, I thought. After filing an application and being accepted, I next had to tell my parents. And so I drove home to Ohio and sat them down one night in the living room. Their reaction was expected, and it seemed almost like a replay of our conversation about entering the convent.

"You'll become a beggar," my father said.

"But Dad—"

"I've never been without a job. Even during the Depression I wouldn't accept handouts. I can't figure how you'd turn your back on a great job in Washington for—"

"For a better thing, Dad."

"For begging money," Mom interjected.

"I feel this is what God wants me to do—to study the Bible, to build a foundation beneath me so I can—"

"So you can stand on a street corner with a tin cup?" Dad asked. "I saw that during the Depression, and I don't want no daughter of mine forgetting her roots and—"

"I'm *strengthening* my roots."

"Deaf, deaf, deaf! I'm telling you I saw beggars, and I'm saying you're making a big mistake. You're not thinking about where you've been and all the struggles we all faced to get you where you are. Don't turn your back on all that. Don't walk away from it. Please. Think about what you're doing."

"I've thought a lot about it, and this is the path I've chosen."

"Well you're not thinking clearly. You're not seeing things right."

"We just see things differently."

"Deaf . . . and blind to boot!" Mom said, her face shouting.

"I don't want to stay in Washington anymore."

"How could you do this? You've worked all your life to have a good job, and we've worked all of our lives to give you that opportunity. Voice lessons, speech lessons, everything. All the private tutoring that made you able to function so me and your mother wouldn't worry about you."

"I'm going to make it. I know I will. But in a different way than you understand."

"Medical insurance, life insurance, you're giving it all up," Mom said. "Who's going to take care of you? We're not going to be around forever to bail you out."

"God will take care of me."

"Don't speak nonsense," Dad said. "You're just going to be a bum. To beg people for money and take handouts."

"No, you're wrong. God is calling me to seminary, and God will take care of my needs."

"God, you say? Do you think so little of your parents? Who do you think has taken care of your needs all these years?"

"God has, through you. I recognize everything that you've done and sacrificed for me. You worked hard, and I wouldn't be where I am today without you. I know all that, and I love you and Mom for all you've done. But it was God who gave you to me and me to you, and maybe now he'll have to provide for me some other way. I don't have the answers or the money or anything else, but I'm not worried because I know if God wants me to go this direction, everything will work out. I'm just going to live by faith."

"Then go ahead. Let God take care of you because you'll not get any help from home. Not a dime."

"I love you, Dad, even though you don't understand."

"You say love, but you don't listen to us," Mom said, turning away. My father joined her, and together they walked out of the room.

As I watched them disappear down the hall and into their bedroom, I knew there was nothing I could say to make them understand. The path I'd now decided to follow was different from what they wanted for me, but I didn't feel I was walking alone. I sensed God's presence right beside me.

17

ROOTS

left for South Carolina on July 4, 1983, minus my dogs, during one of the worst electrical storms in Washington history. As lightning flashed around me and buckets of rain fell from the sky, I was tempted to stay put. But I kept driving through the long, dark, wet night, calming my nerves by singing "Silent Night" mile after mile.

For many hours I didn't see another car on the road. But shortly after I crossed into Georgia, another vehicle materialized as if from nowhere. It was right on my tail and its red lights were flashing. One glance at my speedometer and I knew I was in big trouble.

I pulled over and thought fast. I couldn't afford a ticket. When the state trooper reached my window, I was ready for him.

"Officer, do you have any idea where a rest room is?" I asked with sheer panic in my eyes.

He looked at me real funny and then pointed up the road. "About a mile up ahead," his lips said.

"Oh, thank you, thank you!" Without giving him a chance to say another word, I cranked up my window as fast as I could and took off. In the rearview mirror, I saw him staring after me, as if deciding whether to chase me down. He let me go, and I sang hymns the rest of the way to South Carolina.

I arrived on campus without a cent to my name. Even though I'd already been accepted to school, I didn't know how I could afford the tuition bills. I'd discussed my needs earlier with people in the financial aid office, but no money was available at the time. Nevertheless, I knew that if God wanted me in seminary, he'd have to supply the finances.

That first morning, however, I couldn't register for classes because I didn't have any money. Eager to see what God would do, I again talked with people in the registrar's and financial aid offices, but they had nothing to offer. That afternoon, I was sitting on the steps outside the school when a girl came up and tapped me on the shoulder.

"You're Sue Thomas, aren't you?" she asked. When I nodded, she smiled. "Financial aid wants to see you right away."

When I got to the office, the secretary handed me an envelope. "This just came in the mail for you."

I started to walk out, but she asked me to open the envelope there. When I did, I began to cry. Inside was a check from the Anthony Howe Foundation in Boston to cover my full tuition and book expenses that semester. To me, the gift was as miraculous as anything I'd read in the Bible and confirmed that I was on the right path.

During my entire time at seminary, God continued to meet my needs every step of the way. I saw his blessing when I was hired to work part-time in a campus rehabilitation program and when people left sacks of groceries on my porch. Enabled to attend classes through such generosity, I studied harder than I'd ever studied before.

I was intoxicated with my newfound knowledge about God and the Bible, and I filled my heart with truths that would last a lifetime. With each passing month, I felt the sacrifices I'd made in leaving a secure, prestigious job were all worthwhile. I'd risked much and lost my family's approval, but I gained deep satisfaction from the emotional and spiritual growth I saw in myself.

The greatest lessons were learned outside the classroom. It was in my day-to-day living that I discovered the true meaning of love and friendship and grace, and it was there that the foundation of my future was laid. I made many mistakes and fell back on my insecurities along the way, but I was in a forgiving environment where people saw such things as opportunities for growth and personal development.

As I began to look ahead to what I would do after seminary, I received a lot of advice. Early on, not all of it was particularly welcomed. One day a girl from one of my classes made an offhand comment that I'd make a great missionary to the deaf.

"No, that's the last thing I want to be," I said, somewhat irritated that anybody would claim to know God's will for my life when I didn't even know it. A missionary to the deaf? I would much rather have worked among the poor in Calcutta.

When I heard similar comments from other students and even professors, I became more than irritated—I got mad. After all, I figured God had seen my whole life. He knew every tear I'd ever shed when laughed at or frustrated, as well as the pain I experienced in learning to speak. Having worked so hard to be a part of the hearing world, I couldn't imagine God sending me back to the world of silence.

During my first semester of classes, I met a couple in the bookstore. After we'd been talking awhile, I told them I was deaf and read lips. The woman's jaw dropped.

"That explains everything," she said, laughing.

"Explains what?"

"Well, I sit near you in a couple of classes, and all this time I thought you were a real snob."

"Snob?"

"Because I tried to strike up a conversation with you, but you just ignored me. I had no idea you couldn't hear a word I said!"

The couple invited me to a picnic for grad students later that week and introduced me to many of their friends, most of whom were married. I was quiet at first, as I am when I meet new people. But I was quickly be-friended by one of the couples, Harold and Shirley, who had a comfortable, lived-in appearance about them. They seemed approachable, like the kind of people who worked the showroom floors in the Youngstown Sears store. I imagined he'd be good at selling washers and dryers—talking customers up to the Lady Kenmore for just eight dollars more per month—while she'd be dem-onstrating the self-propelled vacuum cleaners.

Harold and Shirley understood that for me to get to know them, I had to just sit and stare at their faces as they talked. Hearing people can draw close by taking walks or playing games together. But I can't read lips when walking side by side or playing games. I must sit across from somebody and watch their lips. Most people don't have that kind of time, but Harold and Shirley never once looked at their watches.

Right from the start, it seemed as if we'd been lifelong friends. We enjoyed the same foods, liked the same music, laughed at the same jokes. The only difference between us was that I was deaf, but that hardly seemed to matter. With the kind of time we spent together, we discussed and came to understand each other's dreams, fears, insecurities, likes and dislikes, challenges, joys, disappointments, and hopes.

As autumn gave way to winter, we became just like family. Whether studying, grocery shopping, or going to church, we were a regular threesome. Through the spring and even into the summer, if Harold couldn't be with us for some reason, he urged Shirley and me to run along together. I'd never experienced the kind of selfless companionship they offered, and the hardest thing to do each night was say good-bye. I didn't know if they'd still care about me the next morning. But sure enough, Shirley would stop by a couple of days later with a loaf of banana bread or slip an encouraging note into my mailbox.

The autumn of our second year together, they invited me to go camping with them for Thanksgiving. "I've never cooked a turkey outside before," Shirley said, her eyes bright with the excitement of a new challenge. "We can go down to the ocean."

"And barbecue the turkey in one of those fire rings!" I chimed in.

"Exactly! Nothing fancy, but lots of fun!"

"What about equipment? I don't have anything."

"Taken care of. All you have to do is rustle up a sleeping bag. Oh, and bring your van. In a two-person tent, three's a crowd," she said, laughing.

That Thanksgiving on the beach in South Carolina, as Harold chopped wood for the fire and I helped Shirley stuff the turkey, she began to talk about their plans in June after school was out. Her lips said something about moving, something about Wisconsin, something about new opportunities. I glanced away so I wouldn't have to know everything. I wanted to be excited and play the role of a supportive friend, but inside I was bleeding. I didn't want them to leave.

Later, as we gorged ourself on the traditional pilgrims' feast, I was quieter than usual, but they didn't seem to pick up on it. When they finally crawled into their tent and I curled up alone in the back of my van, I felt overcome by an old, familiar emptiness.

Almost from the time we'd met and hit it off so famously, I knew the time would come when our paths would separate. But understanding it mentally and accepting it emotionally were two different things. I'd wrestled with the same thing all of my life: losing the people I grew close to or loved. My brother left home. My skating friend was killed. Soon Harold and Shirley would move away.

The next day as Shirley and I were sitting together on the beach, I felt a growing sense of fear as I thought about losing their companionship. In the coming months as they prepared to leave, they'd get busy. We'd have less time together. The more I mulled it over in my mind, the more anxious I became. I had to do something—anything that could at least keep us closer during the last few months months.

"There's something I need to tell you," I said, turning to face her. I took a deep breath of the salty ocean air and looked deeply into her dark blue eyes. Then I slowly let the breath out. "I don't have much longer to live."

Her hand shot to her mouth.

"I have leukemia, Shirley. I'm dying."

"No, no. . . ." Tears filled her eyes as she struggled to speak. "When did . . . I mean . . . How long have you known?"

"Not long. A couple of weeks."

"But isn't there something . . . *anything* they can do?"

"Normally they'd do transfusions or a marrow transplant. But we didn't catch it in time. It's too late."

Throwing her arms around me, she pulled me close. She looked so genuinely sad that I began crying myself. Hot tears spilled down my cheeks, and the harder I cried the more my body shook. Her arms held me until my tears dried. Finally, I eased away and looked at her squarely.

"These next weeks, maybe months, are going to be hard," I began. "All I want is to have as much time with you and Harold as possible. Quality time."

Unable to talk, she nodded her consent as her eyes again overflowed. With her head on my shoulder, I looked out over the ocean. The yawning mouths of each little wave laughed at me as I sat in my profound silence, overcome with shame for my deception and selfishness.

SUE THOMAS

I tried to contain my lie to just Harold and Shirley.
However, to keep it alive I had to tell others, including
my school advisor. Everybody was equally shocked. I
went through the motions of going to class and taking
tests, but I lived for the time in the evening with Harold and Shirley. Their home was a haven, and they
gave their time and love to me in increasingly gener-
ous portions.

After six long months, the deception began to wear
on me. I tossed and turned through the nights and
sometimes didn't eat for days at a time. Feeling increasingly drawn and haggard, I *looked* sick. But if I was dying from anything, it was from the guilt I felt in having
lied to my friends.

Several times during those long months I started to
tell Shirley that I had lied. But I was afraid of what she
would think. I thought the truth would kill our friendship on the spot. And so I said nothing.

I finally realized I couldn't continue the pretense. I either had to leave the school or face up to the situation I
had created. In my heart, I knew I had to do the hard
thing.

I started by crying out to God and asking his forgiveness. He heard my prayer and gave me the courage to
face Harold and Shirley. After I blurted out the awful
truth to them, I explained that I'd not lied out of malice
but only because the thought of them moving was hard
for me emotionally.

"You were my best friends, and now . . . I won't blame
you if you hate me and never want to see me again," I
said. "But before I go, would you please just call my ad-

visor and tell him I need to see him in the morning. I owe him the truth as well."

After Shirley made that call, she looked me in the face and said, "We'll stand by you. We'll help get you through this."

The following morning, I met with my advisor. I didn't waste any time. As soon as I sat down, I looked at him and said, "For the past six months, I've told a terrible lie. I've told you and some others that I'm dying of leukemia, but I'm not dying at all. I feel awful about it and didn't want to come here, but I owe you an apology and need your forgiveness."

Through my tears, I saw him shake his head with disbelief. And then I saw tears fill his eyes too. He handed me a box of tissue and waited until I composed myself before he said a word.

"I know how hard this must have been for you," he began. "Truth is often painful, but you've done the right thing—and the beautiful thing. There's nothing more beautiful than seeing somebody break the cycle of sin and seek forgiveness. The only thing close is forgiving another. And I give you that assurance now: I do forgive you."

He then gave me the warmest, brightest, friendliest smile I'd seen in a long time. Without averting his gaze, he placed his hand over mine. His smile dimmed.

"There is something that I am now obliged to tell you," he continued. "You have taken the first steps toward restoration, and the next won't be any easier. Our seminary is based on the foundation of truth, as you know. And so it is important that you also inform the academic committee, as well as those whom you involved directly in the lie."

In the days that followed, I sought the forgiveness of twenty-one different students and professors. I thought it would get easier, but each time I wept—not just for my shame but because I realized how deeply I'd hurt people I cared about. I was grateful for Shirley's support during those tough days, though I knew I had to be more independent. She often dropped by at the end of the day to encourage me and tell me she was still my friend.

Two weeks later I went before the academic committee. My nerves were vibrating like piano strings as I entered the room and was guided to a lone chair in the middle of a long table. Breathing a silent prayer, I sat down slowly and placed my Bible in my lap. When I looked up into the bank of faces staring at me, I suddenly felt more ashamed than ever before. Tears flowed from my eyes as I opened my mouth to speak. My tongue felt like a giant hunk of bark inside my mouth, but I forced the words out.

Slowly, very slowly, I took them back to my childhood, explaining that I lost my hearing at about two, and how I felt so separated from the hearing world despite every sacrifice my parents had made to help me fit in. I told them how I'd tried through the years to gain acceptance into their world—by my drinking binges at Ohio State and my fake seizures and then my recent deceit.

"All I wanted was love and attention," I said through my tears. "And I lied to get it. I said I was dying of leukemia, but all along I was just dying from loneliness and insecurity.

"That doesn't excuse my lie," I continued. "It was wrong. I know it was wrong because I couldn't sleep or eat or pray. I couldn't look at myself in the mirror. I thought about running away from the school, but that was the easy way—and I've been that way before. This time I did the hard thing. I confessed my sin and asked forgiveness—of both God and man."

I then opened my Bible and read a passage from Hosea that I'd discovered the night before. The words seemed to have been written just for me. When I substituted my name for the name of Israel, the passage became God's promise to me:

> *Return, O Thomas, to the Lord your God,*
> *For you have stumbled because of your*
> *iniquity.*
> *Return to the Lord, for I will heal your*
> *apostasy,*
> *I will love you freely,*
> *For my anger has turned away from you.*
> *I will be like the dew;*
> *You will blossom like the lily*
> *And take root like the cedars of Lebanon.*

It was as if God was saying, "Look, Thomas, just return to me with all your heart, and I will forgive your sins. Not only that, but I will restore you. Your life will be grounded like the roots of a giant tree. Your life will again have fragrance; you will be renewed."

The men sitting before me sensed the depth of my sorrow. They grieved with me. They prayed with me. And finally they forgave me. I expected justice but was given mercy. When I left, I felt whole and healed. The weight of guilt had been lifted off my shoulders, and the crimson blot on my character had been removed.

To ensure that my restoration was lasting, the academic committee steered me to a well-respected psychologist who helped me understand and then cope with the roots of my problems. He explained that some of my emotions, including loneliness and depression, were entirely normal. A change in routine or even an extra-long night's sleep, he said, was sometimes all that was necessary to turn these emotions around.

He also pointed out, however, that many of my problems had deeper roots. I would always bear the scars from the roller-coaster abuse and trauma I experienced early in life. But those same scars, he said, could enable me to help others overcome their pain—whether they were deaf or hearing.

"Because you are deaf but also have the ability to speak, you straddle the deaf and hearing worlds," he said, sounding almost prophetic. "Your life can be like a bridge between these two worlds, as well as between God and man."

Then he looked at me and added, "You can thank God for new beginnings. He's not finished with you yet, and one day he'll use your life in tremendous ways."

Harold and Shirley eventually moved at the end of the school year as I knew they would. When the time came, I was excited for them and the new adventures they faced in another state, just as I was by the expectancy of seeing where God would lead me. Their departure was still painful, however, and afterward I was once again without close friends. It was back to just God and myself. There was nothing wrong with that, but I kept telling him, "It would be nice to actually *see* your smile and *feel* your arms around me." I sometimes needed that physical affirmation, and it was hard to feel that with God. But I knew he'd somehow fill the void—in his own time and creative way. I just hoped I wouldn't have to wait until I got to heaven.

I was not overly enthusiastic about returning to classes the following semester, but the money kept arriving through various channels to pay my school bills. I laughed at God's sense of humor. Most people want to go to school but don't have the money. I didn't want to go to school, but God kept the money flowing.

I had also asked my church to pray that if God wanted me to stay in school that at least one person would tape and transcribe each of my lectures. The following week, I was surprised when eighteen people volunteered!

After I received the first transcript, I began to cry. Back at Ohio State, I had received lecture notes. But now, for the first time, I had a complete, word-for-word understanding of what was said in the classroom. That very night, I got down on my knees and thanked God for opening the door of understanding to me a little bit farther.

As I prayed, I reflected on earlier years in my life and how I'd received so many special opportunities. There were the speech and music lessons, of course, but also the one-on-one swimming lessons, the restaurant and library excursions, the camp experiences. I'd learned to type and sing and read and skate. And now I was learning about God and having the opportunity to feed my soul.

On my knees at the side of the bed, I then asked that God would use me to somehow open the same doors for other deaf people around the world. I had received so much, but I felt the time had come to begin to give.

In November, I was asked to address the entire student body at a special chapel service dealing with deaf awareness. Unbeknown to me, Bob Coleman, a visiting administrator from the U.S. Center for World Mission, heard about my presentation. Later that night we were introduced, and he asked if I'd be willing to come out to California and begin an organization that would help bridge the gap between the hearing and deaf worlds.

His question stopped me dead in my tracks. I thought about what the psychologist had said earlier about being a bridge, and how various students and professors had talked about me becoming a missionary to the deaf. Hadn't I even prayed about somehow being used in a similar capacity?

I still wasn't convinced. California was on the other side of the planet. I wouldn't know anybody. I'd have no roots.

"No, I don't think so," I said, cutting the conversation short.

"Will you at least sit down and talk to me?"

I saw no harm in at least talking, and so I met with Bob the next day. That led to meetings every day for the entire week, each opening new areas of discussion. The more we talked, the more I began to feel the still, small voice of God inside my heart, urging me to accept the challenge.

"I don't know anything about starting an organization," I said.

"You'll have help from the U.S. Center," he said, explaining that it was a nonprofit resource center linking various missions, whether to the Hindus or Muslims. "Or to the deaf," he added.

"What about housing? I hear it's expensive out there."

"We'll help you find something within your budget."

As time passed, I couldn't ignore the inner sense that perhaps, just perhaps, God was using all the people around me to steer me to California. It seemed so foreign and far away. But wasn't it also the land of opportunity, the place where dreams were supposed to come true?

Finally I gave in and began packing my bags. If God wanted me out west, I was not about to stand in the way. As I loaded my belongings, I worked on the words to a new song: "California, Here I Come."

18

A WEIGHT OF GOLD

arrived in California at two in the morning, tired but full of hope. I slept a few hours in a Pasadena motel and arose with the light of dawn. In my purse I had the address and key of the house that had been prearranged for me, and I was eager to get settled.

When I pulled up to the house, my hopes quickly faded. It looked like a shack in Nicaragua. The exterior hadn't been painted for a dozen years, the wood was rotted, and the yard looked like the aftermath of a guerilla bombing. I had no budget and apparently got a home to match.

After a good long cry, I took a deep breath and got out of my van. If God wanted me in a doghouse, I would make the best of the situation. Careful to avoid the craters in the yard, I walked up to the porch and took out my key. I reached for the handle of the screen door. A screw popped loose and the door pulled off in my hand.

When I finally got inside, the interior looked and smelled like the set of a B-rate thriller. Half expecting the bogeyman or something hairy to jump out of a closet, I screamed when I saw movement in a dark corner. Thankfully, it was just a roach. As it scampered for cover, I threw open some windows to clear the musty fog. Then I got to work, scrubbing and disinfecting and polishing.

A week later, my new home still looked like a shack, but it was the nicest shack in the jungle! There were curtains in the window, fresh paint on the walls, and a shine on every sink and counter. Even the yard had been leveled and seeded. With lots of hard work and bushels of potpourri, I soon had everything smelling like home, sweet home.

Moving in was easy. My belongings consisted of a couch and a few suitcases. I slept on the floor. Exhausted from cleaning, I collapsed into "bed" and was quickly sound asleep. In the middle of the night, I felt a faraway sensation that the floor was rocking and swaying. I smiled in my sleep, thinking I was dreaming of a waterbed. When I finally opened my eyes, I was still rocking. It wasn't a dream. It was an earthquake!

Having nobody around and knowing nothing about earthquakes, I was terrified. A special teletype phone had been installed for my use, so I crawled across the floor and picked up the receiver. In the pitch black of night, I called the relay operator.

"Can you tell me, did we just experience an earthquake?" I typed.

"You bet. It was a biggie," came the transmission.

"What do I do?"

"Just go back to sleep."

"No, I mean what do I *do?* Is this the Big One or is the Big One still coming?"

"That's the end of it. Just go back to sleep."

As I signed off to end the conversation, I wondered what kind of a nut I was dealing with. How could anybody just go back to sleep? I stayed awake the whole night, wondering if the house would cave in atop me and questioning why I'd ever agreed to move to California in the first place.

Once my rattled nerves had settled, I slowly began to acclimate to my new surroundings. The U.S. Center for World Mission helped me gather necessary furniture for my home and provided me with my first office. I had a sign made for the door and stationery printed. I was now Sue Thomas, president of Operation SOUND. I'd thought of the name on the way out to California, and it had a nice ring to it. As far as titles go, I'd thought about naming myself Supreme Allied Commander, but president seemed more humble. However, once the preliminaries were taken care of, I was stumped. I didn't know what to do next.

Some early encouragement and inspiration was provided by Joni Eareckson Tada, a young quadriplegic who had successfully launched Joni and Friends, an organization focused on the needs of the disabled. I also sought the advice of Paul Cedar, pastor of Lake Avenue Congregational Church, which I had started attending. When I finished telling him who I was and my dreams for Operation SOUND, he wrote a name on a slip of paper. It was an attorney in nearby Arcadia named William Hahn.

"Go to Willie, tell him I sent you, and see what God does."

The very next day, I showed up at the legal office and Willie heard me out. After I'd told him my entire life saga and where I was headed, I was encouraged that he was still awake. I looked at him and he looked at me. Then he smiled and said, "When do we start?"

A bearded, gentle man, Willie graciously handled all of the legal documents to get me started and agreed to serve as chairman of my board of directors. Other board members soon joined us, and together we slowly began to build the bridge between the hearing and deaf worlds.

I spoke wherever I was invited—at first just to small groups here and there. At each gathering, whether it was to the deaf or hearing, I talked candidly of the struggles I faced, the obstacles I overcame, the mistakes I made, and the hope and forgiveness I finally experienced from God during my darkest hour. Often I ended by singing "Silent Night."

That beautiful song, so dear to me, represented much of my life story. "Silent" because of my deafness; "Night" because of my separation from God. Later it came to signify my celebration of Christ's birth and the joy of my relationship with God. Apart from God, nothing else really made much sense. With him, I discovered meaning and purpose and hope.

Everywhere I spoke, the response was overwhelming. One contact led to another, and soon I was traveling back and forth across the country, speaking at various schools, churches, hospitals, and civic organizations, as well as on television and radio. Through my life, people began to understand the unique needs of the deaf—as well as God's ability to help them overcome the barriers in their own lives. The bridge was being built!

As far as my need for companionship, God met that in his own time and creative way, as I suspected he would. Before I'd left for California, the dean of women at the seminary handed me an article she'd read about Hearing Ear dogs. "You know, you really should think about getting one to help you," she said.

I didn't read it until the following Sunday when an elderly woman gave me the same clipping at church. I then wrote to the American Humane Society for a list of Hearing Ear dog programs, and soon thereafter filed an application with Dogs for the Deaf in Jacksonville, Oregon.

Because the dogs were all strays from area Humane Society pounds, I knew I couldn't be too picky about my preference of animals. In the end, I would have been happy with a toy poodle. But I asked for a golden retriever, a dog I could wrap my arms around.

After waiting and praying several long months, I was notified that a golden retriever had been located—but not to get my hopes up. Because the dog had been badly abused, he was shy and cowardly, and they weren't sure he was trainable. They said his attention span was short and that, rather than work, he'd roll over at the trainer's feet.

With love and patience, he began to respond and even excel at training. A year later, when it appeared that my dream dog would become a reality, they finally told me his name: Levi. My seminary professor said the name meant "attached to" in Hebrew. I liked the strong, biblical name and figured Levi would, by becoming my ears, be as *attached to* me as he could possibly get.

The day Levi arrived, a month after I landed in California, I was as nervous as a new mother. But all my anxieties and fears disappeared when seventy-six pounds of floppy-eared, tail-wagging love barreled out of the trainer's van. With tears in my eyes, I kneeled down and wrapped my arms around him as he gave me a big dog smile and licked my face. At that moment, the tremendous void was filled in my life. I knew he'd give me the companionship I needed, while I'd provide him with the love he never had as a puppy.

For the first week, the trainer stopped by each morning to help me learn what she'd spent the past year teaching Levi. The rest of the day and night, Levi and I got acquainted and acclimated to each other. From the start, I was amazed at his ability to alert me to such sounds as the telephone, oven timer, doorbell, or smoke alarm. He was even able to summon me if somebody said, "Hey, Levi, go get Sue."

What I didn't realize was how much Levi would open my world. Before he arrived, I never knew when somebody was knocking on the door or ringing the doorbell. My friends had to schedule appointments, and if they said they'd come by at two o'clock, I'd begin waiting by the window five minutes beforehand. If they were late, I couldn't move. If I wasn't looking outside, I'd miss them, and all the noise in the world wouldn't get my attention.

A week after Levi arrived, I discovered just how seriously he took his job. Early one morning as I was bathing, he suddenly burst through the bathroom door. He'd been trained to alert me to sounds in a very physical way. If I was sitting down and the phone rang, he lunged into my lap and then ran back to the sound. If I was standing up, he practically knocked me down.

When he saw me in the bath, however, he hesitated. He eyeballed the sides of the tub for a split second, and the next thing I knew Old Faithful leaped right into the water with me!

"It's OK, Levi!" I said, trying to push him out. But he just thrashed about atop me until I finally stood up, grabbed a towel and robe, and followed him to the door.

Never before had my bath been interrupted by somebody at the door. I thought, *This is what it's like to be hearing! People are constantly interrupted by sounds.* When I finally got back into the tub, I'd no sooner sat down than Levi plunged into the tub again—because of a ringing phone. He took a third dive for another phone call ten minutes later.

Exasperated, I climbed out and went eyeball to eyeball with Levi. "I never knew I had it so good without you!"

The days of sleeping through the night were also over. Late one night he jumped onto the bed with me but seemed confused about where to lead me. I got up, but there was nobody on the phone or at the door. The oven timer was shut off, and no fire had triggered the smoke alarm. When I felt a sudden vibration rise up through my feet, I suspected thunder. I walked over to the window and looked outside. Sure enough, rain was beating against the window.

"Thank you, Levi," I said groggily. "Thank you for waking me up to tell me there's a storm outside."

I soon discovered he was the best alarm clock in the world. Before he arrived I used a flashing light contraption my father had devised. If I didn't feel like getting up, I merely reached over, turned it off, and drifted back to sleep. However, Levi wouldn't put up with snoozing. He leaped into bed with the first hint of the alarm, nosed my head, and then licked my face until I acknowledged his presence. He was happy and wanted to play, and his excitement was contagious. With Levi around, it was impossible to wake up without a smile on my face!

Along with joy, he also brought a tremendous sense of security into my life. Before he arrived, I was frequently scared at night. Knowing I couldn't hear if somebody tried to break in, I always prayed before bedtime, asking God to guard my doors and windows with a legion of angels. When Levi appeared on the scene, God's angels got a break.

He was a perfect guard dog, and before long I could tell what he was hearing. When I was cross-stitching at night, his ears sometimes perked up and he'd lift his head off my feet and look around sleepily. His groggy eyes told me that all was well. Other times he'd bolt upright and fly to the door. When I let him out, he generally stayed out just long enough to scare off a cat.

One time, however, he darted back a few minutes later and began wiping his nose on the carpet. Thinking he might have been clawed, I put my face down for a closer look. All of a sudden, the smell hit me like a freight train. The odor was so thick I could practically see it.

"Levi, that wasn't a cat!" I scolded. "It was a skunk!"

I'd read somewhere that the only way to neutralize the smell of a skunk was with tomato juice. So I made a quick dash to the corner grocery store. When I returned, I dragged Levi into the bathtub and poured four cans into his fur. Everything went smoothly—until he decided to shake off. A moment later, my bathroom looked like the scene of a Rambo massacre.

Despite my efforts, I couldn't get the smell out of his coat. It stayed with him for more than a week, during which he wanted a double dose of love and affection. One night he crawled up beside me on the pillow. One breath and I was wide awake.

"I love you, Levi, but you're testing my limits!" I said, shoving and pushing him off the bed.

Shortly after Levi's break-in training was completed, I was invited to speak before a large out-of-state gathering. If he was to share the spotlight, I wanted him to look his best. So I took him to a groomer and had him bathed, clipped, and his nails cut.

Though he looked great, he was still untested before a large audience, and I was unsure how he'd respond. At the airport, I made a quick rest-room stop prior to boarding. I used the handicapped stall because it was large enough for Levi to lie down at my feet. When his tail began wagging furiously, I smiled—but only for a moment. The next thing I knew, he nosed beneath the partition and was off visiting people in adjoining stalls!

That didn't ease my anxiety when we finally boarded the plane. By law, Hearing Ear dogs are allowed in the cabin, but I was skittish about how he'd behave. When lunch was served, would he hop up and gobble down the lunch of a nearby passenger? If I fell asleep, would he wander off? Would he whine and whimper and shake like a leaf? Thankfully, my fears were unfounded.

Levi walked aboard as if born on a plane, lay down at my feet, and stayed there the entire trip.

During the flight, he was a magnet to fellow dog lovers. People made a beeline to him, and I didn't get a moment's rest. Fellow passengers constantly asked, "How did you get your dog on board? We've been trying for years." I explained that he was a Hearing Ear dog. Then they asked where I was going and what I did, which enabled me to tell them about Operation SOUND and my life story. As the discussions spilled over into God's love and forgiveness, I often felt as if the holiest place in the world was right there in the cabin as we cruised along at 35,000 feet.

When we eventually arrived at the Hyatt Hotel where the engagement was scheduled, I was awed by the lavish crystal and marble in the lobby. I winked at Levi. "God has taken us on an amazing journey—from the doghouse to the penthouse!"

At the end of my talk, I told the people I wanted to introduce them to my closest friend and constant travel companion—one who received a stay of execution just three days before he was scheduled to die. Purposely vague, I knew they thought I was hanging out with some jailbird from San Quentin. But they erupted with applause when Levi suddenly darted down the aisle from the back of the hall, leaped onto the stage, and nearly bowled me over. That day, a star was born. A hunk of retriever, he's worth his weight in gold!

19

LOOKING HOMEWARD

As I look back on those early months of Operation SOUND, and the many years before that, I can see God's guidance and blessing throughout my life. There were some rough roads, and I know there will be more ahead. But with him leading the way and with Levi at my side, I will continue working to help break the sound barrier. Together, this will be our job until the day of glory.

When the organization was first launched, I had no idea where the path would lead. Who would listen to a young deaf woman? What could people, whether they could hear or not, possibly gain from the example of a solitary life lived in total silence since infancy? Could God prompt positive results from what many people would consider a human tragedy?

These were real concerns, and I honestly didn't know the answers. But the more people I met, the more I realized that my handicap was no greater than others'— even those who have the full use of all their senses but who nevertheless do not take the time to communicate, to interact, to *feel* what others feel. I also discovered how few people actually *hear* what others say, or can distinguish the still, small voice of God from amidst the clatter and clamor of daily living. It's because I've heard his voice that I've been able to overcome very real barriers in life and help others do the same.

When I look back on all that I have gone through, I realize that it is a remarkable journey. I see my story as one of victory, of hope, of gratitude for what God has done in my life. Although some people believe that homosexuality is not curable, my life today is a testimony that God can do amazing things in people's lives if they allow him. But it has to be their heartfelt desire; they have to allow that transformation to take place. It's not that my homosexual impulses have been silenced or just put in the background. They are gone; my life has been transformed.

Going before the elders of the seminary to confess my deception was really the turning point in my life. When I went before these men, I was overwhelmed with guilt and shame. My confession and their forgiveness began a restoring process through which I have found freedom. Through this I have learned that confession not only deals with past sins but works as a safeguard against further sin because of the accountability to others.

When I travel I must travel alone with my dog. As an unmarried woman, I wouldn't travel with a man, and because of where I have been in the past I cannot travel with a woman. God has brought my dog into my life to give me the companionship and protection I need. I will protect in every way the healing and the reputation God has given me.

Negative factors dealing with males in my childhood probably led me down the path toward homosexuality in the beginning—the torment and laughter of boys, abuse by an older man, my brother leaving home. I'm not making excuses, because I have come to understand that what I did was in rebellion against God's purpose for man and woman. I have peace now in being able to enjoy the company of both men and women. This victory comes through growth, through total healing.

I came to a place of lasting change because of God's promise to me in those words from Hosea—that his anger had turned away from me, that I would blossom like a lily, that I would flourish like a giant cedar. I believed those words, and it was a beautiful promise, so deep and powerful that I don't want to do anything to interrupt my open relationship with God ever again.

This promise wasn't just for me. I can identify with people who are out there doing their own thing because I too spent years trying to satisfy my own needs without reference to what God wanted for my life. I can also relate to them in their pain, their anguish, their awareness that they are not fulfilled. I just want to be able to reach out to them with that promise and say, "Here, take it—it's for you! Wherever you are, you don't have to be there. You can come back."

Of course, my life today is not entirely free from struggles. One of the difficulties is caused by my skill in lipreading. Many people, even close friends, tell me that

I'm so much like a hearing person. I appreciate that, but it's frustrating to realize that hearing people can't even imagine what it's like to be deaf. I spend my whole life seeing movement but never hearing a sound.

And that is the pain that is always with me. I would give anything to be able to hear life. When I go to the ocean and see the waves crashing on the shore, I see their power, but I can't hear them. In the woods I see the trees moving with the wind, and I wonder what they sound like. People try but are unable to describe those sounds. This is a void that cannot be filled. Sure, God gives strength and peace, even the kind that buffers and gets me through the worst imaginable problems. But I would be both unrealistic and dishonest to pretend that I have no anguish there.

I am used to breaking out of my silent world by using the relay phone system. But here is probably my biggest complaint to God. Why do I always have to go to hearing people? Why can't they come to me? There have been times when I have been sick, and it would have been so neat to have somebody call me up just to say, "Hi, how are you doing? I just called to see how your day is going." Then I would be able to tell them how I feel. I think that's what happens in normal friendships. But since people don't call me, I struggle with whether to make a phone call to say that I'm feeling lousy. I know for hearing people it's more time consuming to call a deaf person using the relay phone system. I understand this, but it's still a struggle.

Sometimes I handle this pain by speaking before churches and other groups, trying to get them to do something to make a better world for the deaf. On those occasions I handle it with boldness and truth. Other times I handle it alone through prayer or singing hymns. And then there are the days when I don't handle it! On those days I'm not fit to live with. I pout and mumble and grumble to God. But when I come through those times I find that God was carrying me along—even when I didn't realize it.

God allowed me to become deaf, and I honestly believe that it is for his glory. If I had to re-enter the world and be deaf all over again, I would be content in that. This is really the growth in my life, coming to understand and be content with the lot he has given me. There is such a peace in knowing that he is in control, and so I don't have to despair but can face life with courage. In spite of those painful days, I can still have the joy.

I want to stay exactly where I am in my relationship with God. But I also know that there is a higher place, a deeper meaning, and I want to search for that in my relationship with him. I want to learn as much as I can so I can give it to others. I feel unique and very privileged. God not only died for me, but he took the time to heal me and to use me.

Many people today don't feel they can be used by God. They just struggle with everything. I want everyone to feel they are unique and that their lives matter to God. He wants them to come home, to give him the chance to transform and heal, and then—when they least expect it—to use them.

I am happy to report that my parents are doing well although they're into their seventies and eighties. They have celebrated over fifty years of married life together.

All three of my brothers grew up to be men that I respect and appreciate. Each of them has two children.
Billy has grown closer to the family over the years.
Paul—the one who spent all of his time in the woods
hunting and becoming a self-made taxidermist—still
spends all of his time in the woods! The one difference
is that now he is in demand as an internationally famous taxidermist. Bob and I have yet to grow up: we
still punch each other every time we get together. We
all have special times when the family is reunited.

Mom is doing great. Sharing in this book about her
struggles has been a difficult thing to do, and she has
felt unsure about exactly how people would respond. I
encouraged her to see that the world wasn't going to
judge and condemn her for her past. Every one of us
must be accountable to look deep inside to see that we
all have been affected by our sin nature. In a sense this
book is Mom's story, too, because she has opened herself and shared her wounds so that others might know
that victory is possible.

In the final stages of this book, Mom told me for the
first time about her own childhood experiences and the
pain she suffered. That was an overwhelming experience for me, having a woman at the age of seventy-
seven, with tears streaming down her face, return to
her childhood. I saw that my mother is a person, with
real hurts and needs, just as I am. I learned that the
deep pain she experienced in adulthood was not
caused by my deafness. It had been carried from her
childhood and never dealt with.

Working on this book has also begun a healing process for our family as a whole. People considered us to

be a typical, healthy family. And we were typical: we were a family that had joys and problems. I've come to realize that most families do. We didn't have any major tragedies, but there was enough heartache for me to understand feelings of pain both in myself and in others. And now as some of our family's tender spots are out in the open, we can talk about them without fear.

The only thing I blame myself for in regard to my parents is that as a child I didn't appreciate all of their sacrifice and giving. I care a lot about that now. As I reflect back I understand that my dad took on many extra jobs to pay for my training. And every time my mother sat me down in front of the mirror for speech therapy, every time she took me to the skating rink, every time I fought with her because I didn't want to do what I was made to do, she would look gently down into my face and say those now famous words: *Someday you're going to thank me*. And how right she was!

Without the tremendous sacrifice and love of my parents, there wouldn't even be a story for me to tell. I've gained a great love and respect for my mother and father. I now look at both of my parents as my best friends. They are unwavering in their love and support, and they always will be. I would pray that anyone who reads these pages or meets me personally would sense my gratitude for my family and appreciation for their support.

I will continue to use my voice to help bridge the gap between the hearing and deaf worlds. My life is dedicated to that, as long as I have breath in my body—or until that day when Gabriel raises his heavenly trumpet and calls the saints home. I like to think I will be the first to hear that golden note when the sound barrier is finally and forever broken, and that Levi will follow right behind me as I am ushered through heaven's gate. At that moment, the deaf will hear, the lame will walk, and the mute will speak. In the twinkling of an eye, all of the tears will be dried, and words such as "I'm sorry" and "good-bye" will be heard for the very last time.

It will be a day of restoration, joyful reunion, and unspeakable glory. However, there is no time to celebrate now, because my job on earth is not yet done. On that day when Gabriel sounds his clarion call, I don't want to go alone. I want to be surrounded by legions of family and friends who, like me, will hear God's words—yes, actually *hear* his commendation, "Well done, my good and faithful servant!"

On that day of glory, perhaps I'll ask God to replay for me the songs I missed along the way—the song of falling rain, a baby's laughter, and tumbling brooks; of church bells ringing, ocean waves crashing, and roosters crowing. And then I will repay the favor by raising my voice on high, as heavenly hosts sing *Alleluia*. On that day, my silence will be filled with a new song, and the night will give way to eternal dawn.